KT-117-617

THE  TIMES

BOOK OF IQ TESTS

top uk mensa puzzle editors

ken russell and philip carter

book 1

KOGAN
PAGE

First published in 2001
Reprinted 2001

Apart from any fair dealing for the purposes of research or private study, or criticism or review, as permitted under the Copyright, Designs and Patents Act 1988, this publication may only be reproduced, stored or transmitted, in any form or by any means, with the prior permission in writing of the publishers, or in the case of reprographic reproduction in accordance with the terms and licences issued by the CLA. Enquiries concerning reproduction outside these terms should be sent to the publishers at the undermentioned address:

Kogan Page Limited
120 Pentonville Road
London
N1 9JN

© Ken Russell and Philip Carter, 2001

The right of Ken Russell and Philip Carter to be identified as the authors of this work has been asserted by them in accordance with the Copyright, Designs and Patents Act 1988.

The views expressed in this book are those of the authors, and are not necessarily the same as those of Times Newspapers Ltd.

British Library Cataloguing in Publication Data

A CIP record for this book is available from the British Library.

ISBN 0 7494 3473 2

Typeset by Jean Coussons Typesetting, Diss, Norfolk
Printed and bound in Great Britain by Clays Ltd, St Ives plc

Contents

Introduction

Intelligence is the capacity to learn or understand. Every person possesses a single general ability of mind. This general ability varies in amount from person to person, but remains approximately the same throughout life for any individual.

'IQ' stands for Intelligence Quotient. The definition of quotient is 'the number of times one quantity is contained in another'. Intelligence can be defined as 'mental ability, quickness of mind'.

When the IQ of a child is being measured, the child attempts an intelligence test that has been standardized, with the average score recorded for each age group. Thus, a child of 8 years of age who successfully passed a test for a child of 10 years of age would have an IQ of 10 divided by 8 and multiplied by 100, thus: $1.25 \times 100 = 125$. A child of 8 years of age who successfully passed a test for a child of 8, but failed a test for a child of 9 would have an IQ of 8 divided by 8, times 100: $1 \times 100 = 100$, which is the norm.

Because mental age remains constant in development to about the age of 13, and then gradually slows up to the age of 18, after which little or no improvement is found, adults have to be judged on an IQ test whose average score is 100, and their results graded above and below this norm according to known scores.

Although it is generally agreed that IQ is hereditary and

remains fairly constant throughout life, it is possible to improve one's performance on IQ tests. We believe that, by practising different types of questions you may encounter, it is possible to improve by a few vital percentage points.

IQ tests are set and used on the assumption that those taking the test have no knowledge of the testing method itself and that they know very little about the question methods within these tests. Logically, therefore, it follows that if you learn something about this form of testing and know how to approach the different kinds of question you can improve your performance on the tests themselves. It is this improvement in performance that this book sets out to achieve.

The tests that follow have been newly compiled for this book and are not, therefore, standardized, so an actual IQ assessment cannot be given. However, there is a guide below to assessing your performance at the end of each test, and there is also a cumulative guide for your overall performance on all 10 tests.

A time limit of 90 minutes is allowed for each test. The correct answers are given at the end of each test, and you should award yourself one point for each correct answer. Calculators may be used to assist with solving numerical questions if preferred.

You can assess your performance as follows:

One test

Score	Rating
36–40	Exceptional
31–35	Excellent
25–30	Very good
19–24	Good
14–18	Average

Ten tests

Score	Rating
351–400	Exceptional
301–350	Excellent
241–300	Very good
181–240	Good
140–180	Average

Test One: Questions

1. Which word in brackets is closest in meaning to the word in capitals?

   IRREFUTABLE (lost, sure, wise, secure, optimal)

2.

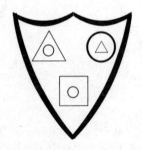

Which shield below is most like the shield opposite?

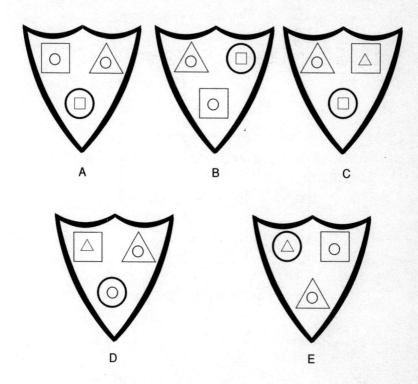

A

B

C

D

E

3. Insert three body parts (each three letters long) into the gaps to complete the words below:

W _ _ _ Y
E _ _ _ Y
T _ _ _ E

4. What number should replace the question mark?

7	5	6	6
5	4	3	4
2	9	4	?

5. Which is the odd one out?

    transcend, cascade, plummet, subside, prolapse

6.

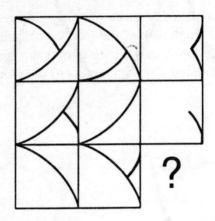

    Which square should replace the question mark?

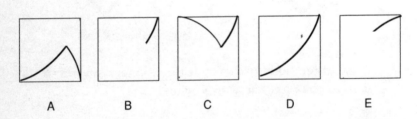

    A   B   C   D   E

7. Only one of the following groups of five letters can be arranged to form an English five-letter word. Can you find the word?

    MURDC
    BEWAP
    UNREL
    YIGEN
    THABL

8. Insert a word in the brackets that means the same as the definitions outside the brackets.

   lightly-built (   ) give offence to

9. A train travelling at a speed of 90 mph enters a tunnel 3.5 miles long. The length of the train is 0.25 miles. How long does it take for all of the train to pass through the tunnel, from the moment the front enters to the moment the rear emerges?

10. auri- is to gold as argent- is to:

    brass, steel, emerald, silver, aluminium

11.

What comes next in the above sequence?

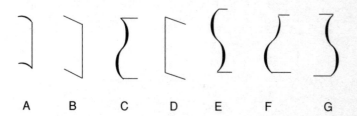

  A   B   C   D   E   F   G

12. What number should replace the question mark?

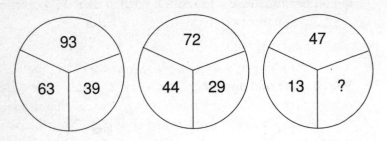

13. Which phrase in brackets is opposite to the phrase in capitals?

    AS A RULE (out of turn, hardly ever, out of date, rough-and-ready, now and again)

14. What number should replace the question mark?

15. In the sequence below, which letter is two to the right of the letter, immediately to the left of the letter, three to the right of the letter, two to the left of the letter D?

    A B C D E F G H

16. Which is the odd one out?

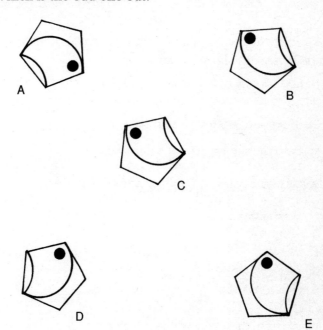

17. What letter should replace the question mark?

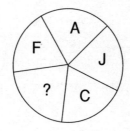

18. What phrase is suggested by the arrangement of letters below?

$$
\begin{array}{ccccccc}
 & & & C & & & \\
 & O & & & N & & \\
 & F & & E & & R & \\
E & & N & & C & & E
\end{array}
$$

19. Which word when inserted in the brackets will complete the first word and start the second?

    IMP (_ _ _) EAR

20. Harbour is to shelter as nurture is to:

    shield, rear, secure, pamper, immunize

21. What is the meaning of fastigate?
    a. doubled
    b. slippery
    c. closed
    d. like a pyramid
    e. 5-barred gate

22. Place two three-letter bits together to make a six-letter word.

    ING ETS LOW LIN DAF SWA MER NER ROB ODI
    Clue: bird.

23. All of the vowels are missing from this trite saying, 'Hood's Warning'. Can you replace them?

    BSRTH BRNSN GGDBF RPTTN GTHMT HNGR

24. What four-letter word is missing in this list?

    palm
    mast
    tory

    _ _ _ _
    ante
    earn
    nose

25. Which number should replace the question mark?

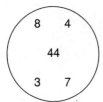 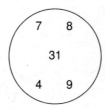 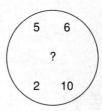

26. See if you can rearrange these words to make a trite saying.

LIBRARY	A	LIKE	BY
TO	READ	A	COLLECT
WOMAN	HE	TIME	CAN
IS	THE	TOO	A
MAN	A	BOOK	OLD

27.

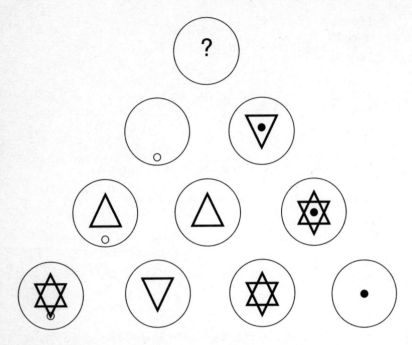

Which circle should replace the question mark?

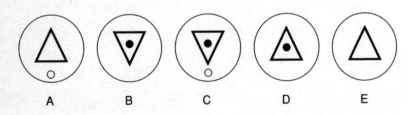

| A | B | C | D | E |

28. What is the name for a group of goats?

    a. lepe
    b. flock
    c. rush
    d. sounder

29. Fill in the blanks to find a word.

30. What have all of these words in common?

   pond
   toga
   seal
   find
   joan
   spin

31. Place two four-letter bits together to make an eight-letter word.

   PEDI BURT GIGA FRAI ETIK NTIC PHON LING CUBB LICY

32. What number should replace the question mark?

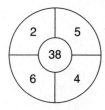 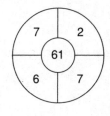 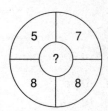

33. Fill in the letters to spell out two fish of six letters.

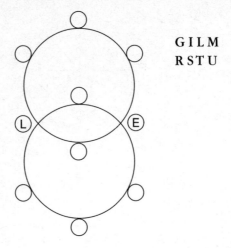

GILM
RSTU

34.

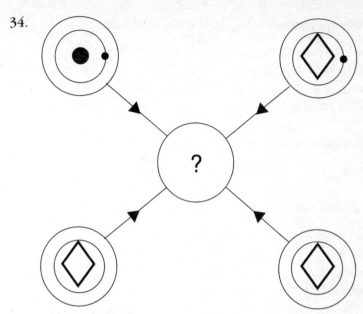

Each line and symbol that appears in the four outer circles, above, is transferred to the centre circle according to these rules. If a line or symbol occurs in the outer circles:

once: it is transferred
twice: it is possibly transferred
3 times: it is transferred
4 times: it is not transferred

Which of the circles A, B, C, D or E, shown below, should appear at the centre of the diagram, above?

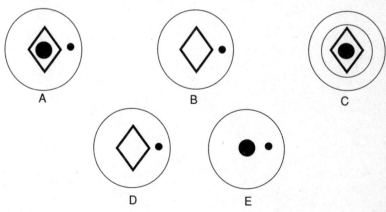

15

35. What is medulla?

    a. bone marrow
    b. a medal
    c. a star
    d. a module

36. Replace the vowels to form a word:

    C R P C

37. What is an orris?

    a. pepper
    b. horse
    c. flower
    d. architrave

38. Insert a word in the brackets that means the same as the words outside the brackets.

    GEM (_ _ _ _ _ _) DUNG BEETLE

39. Which one of B will not fit into A to make six-letter words?

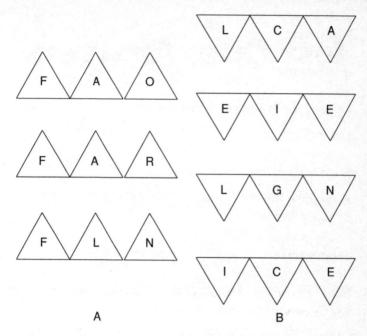

A

B

40. Find a boxing term made up of six letters outside the star and six letters inside the star.

Test One: Answers

1. sure

2. E; it contains a triangle in a circle, a circle in a square and a circle in a triangle.

3. ear, leg and rib, to make weary, elegy and tribe.

4. 5; add the first three numbers in each row, then divide by 3 to obtain the final number: $2 + 9 + 4 = 15/3 = 5$.

5. transcend; all the other words relate to fall. Transcend is a word relating to rise.

6. B; the contents of the final square in each horizontal and vertical line is determined by the contents of the first two squares. Lines are carried forward from the first two squares to the final square, except where two lines appear in the same position, in which case they are cancelled out.

7. YIGEN = eying

8. slight

9. 2 mins 30 seconds;

   $((3.5 + 0.25) \times 60/90)$ minutes $= 3.75 \times 60/90 = 2.5$ mins or 2 mins 30 secs.

10. silver

11. E; the first four complete figures are being repeated in the same order but only the left half is shown.

12. 15. Add the top and left-hand numbers and divide by 4: $47 + 13 = 60/4 = 15$.

13. hardly ever

14. 5; looking down columns from left to right, $96 + 427 = 523$

15. F

16. D; the rest are all the same figure rotated.

17. O. Start at A and jump to alternate segments working clockwise in the sequence: AbCdeFghiJklmO.

18. summit conference

19. end: to give impend and endear.

20. rear

21. d. like a pyramid

22. merlin

23. Be sure the brain is engaged before putting the mouth in gear.

24. Yoga. The first letter of each word is the same as the last letter of the preceding word.

25. $38; (8 \times 7 = 56) - (3 \times 4 = 12) = 44; (7 \times 9 = 63) - (4 \times 8 = 32) = 31; (5 \times 10 = 50) - (2 \times 6 = 12) = 38$

26. By the time a man can read a woman like a book he is too old to collect a library.

27. C; each pair of circles is added together to produce the circle above, but similar symbols disappear.

28. b. flock

29. disgorge

30. The first two letters start the name of a country and the last two letters finish the name: POLAND, TONGA, SENEGAL, FINLAND, JORDAN, SPAIN

31. gigantic

32. $96; (6 \times 5) + (2 \times 4) = 38; (6 \times 2) + (7 \times 7) = 61; (8 \times 7) + (5 \times 8) = 96$

33. mullet, grilse

34. A

35. a. bone marrow

36. carapace

37. c. flower

38. scarab

39. LCA. The others make: flagon, fiacre, feline.

40. bantam-weight

Test Two: Questions

1. How many minutes is it before 12 noon if 15 minutes ago it was four times as many minutes past 9 am?

2. If meat in a river (3 in 6) is T(ham)es, find a word meaning *contented* in a country (4 in 10).

3. Which two words are most alike in meaning?

   boycott, litigate, proscribe, sanction, postulate, intend

4.

Which shield should replace the question mark?

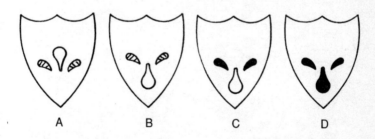

A   B   C   D

5. 'How many steps to the top of the Eiffel Tower?' asked the tourist. '896 steps plus half the number of steps,' replied the gendarme. How many steps are there to the top of the Eiffel Tower?

6. Complete the three words so that the last two letters of the first word are the first two letters of the second word, the last two letters of the second word are the first two letters of the third word, and the last two letters of the third word are the first two letters of the first word, thus completing the circle:

_ _ M P _ _
_ _ M I _ _
_ _ G A _ _

7. Which two words that sound alike but are spelt differently mean pure/hunted?

8.

 is to:

as:

is to:

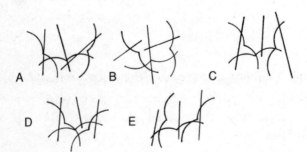

9. Which is the odd one out?

   artful, astute, shifty, devious, guileful

10. Insert the letters of the phrase: RAVISH TAIL once each only into the blanks to complete two words which mean the same as the words above them:

        wait   pertinent
     _E_ _T_ _E _E_ _T_ _E

11. Which two letters should replace the question mark?

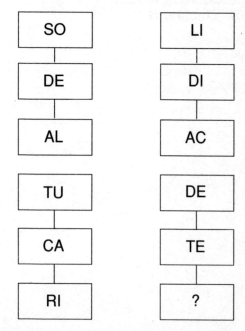

SO   LI
DE   DI
AL   AC
TU   DE
CA   TE
RI   ?

12. What number should replace the question mark?

72	(68)	41
28	(98)	16
34	(??)	56

13. Martinmas is to November as Candlemas is to:

    January, February, March, October, December

14. A well-known phrase has been divided into groups of three letters that have then been placed in the wrong order. Find the phrase:

    EST HON OBI LTW ONE RDS WIT KIL

15. Find one word in List B that should be placed with the words in List A to replace the question mark.

List A	List B
tape	chip
wood	bell
wine	card
deer	bottle
flag	note
?	

16.

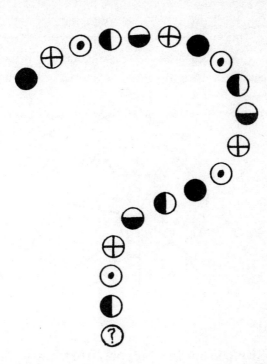

Which circle below should replace the circle with the
question mark?

A　　B　　C　　D　　E

17. Which two words are the odd ones out?

end	use	domains	precast
rub	can	sadness	met
ace	suburbs	panache	ice
presume	special	attempt	aim

18. What number should replace the question mark?

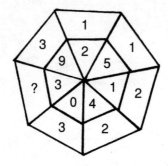

19. Which word in brackets is opposite to the word in capitals?

    MOTLEY (sensible, uniform, smooth, sweet, saturnine)

20. Which is the odd one out?

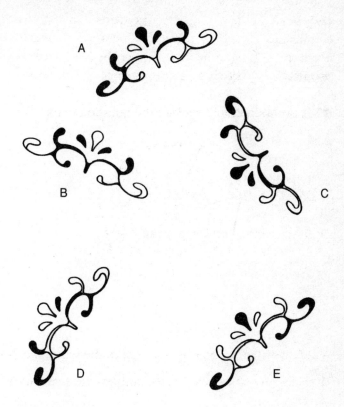

21. What is a lateen?

    a. a musical instrument
    b. a bishop's hat
    c. a sail
    d. a bird

22. What is the name given to a group of flies?

    a. hover
    b. muster
    c. knob
    d. grist

23. What is pompano?

    a. fish
    b. grapefruit
    c. grapes
    d. bread

24. Find the missing letters to make a word.

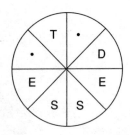

25. Fill in the letters to make two dogs of six letters each.

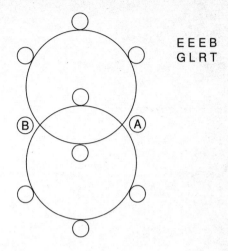

E E E B
G L R T

26. What number should replace the question mark?

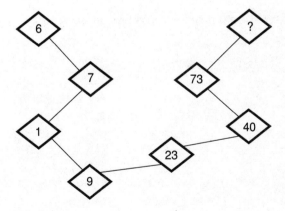

27.

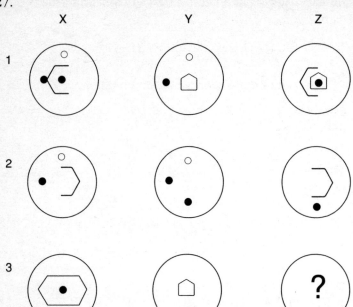

Which letter should replace the question mark to a definite rule?

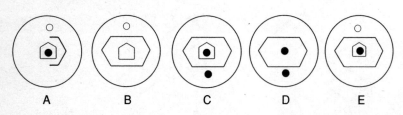

28. Which of the following is always associated with entrecote?

a. eels
b. cream
c. rice
d. steak

29. All the vowels have been removed from this trite saying, 'Sukhomlinov's Law'.

    THMST BRLLN TLYDR SSDRM YWLLS LLYLS

30. What do all of these words have in common?

    calmness
    undefended
    firstly
    sighing
    disturb

31. What five-letter word can be placed in front of each of these words to make new words?

    _ _ _ _ _ BIRD
    _ _ _ _ _ CLUB
    _ _ _ _ _ FALL
    _ _ _ _ _ JAR
    _ _ _ _ _ SCHOOL

32. What number should replace the question mark?

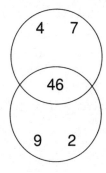 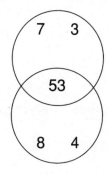 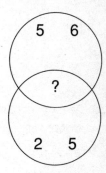

33. Find the 10-letter word by moving from circle to circle; each circle must be only used once.

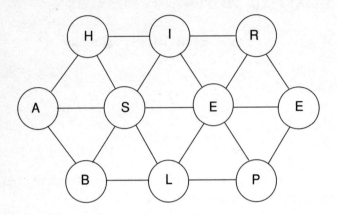

34.

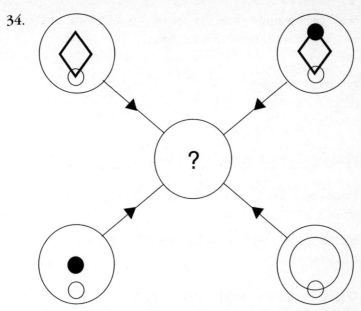

Each line and symbol that appears in the four outer circles, above, is transferred to the centre circle according to these rules. If a line or symbol occurs in the outer circles:

once: it is transferred
twice: it is possibly transferred
3 times: it is transferred
4 times: it is not transferred

Which of the circles A, B, C, D or E, shown below, should appear at the centre of the diagram, above?

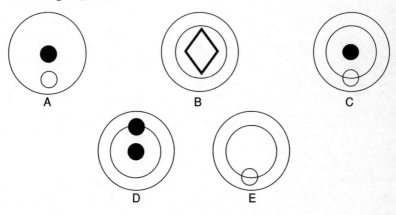

35. What is grosgrain?

    a. food
    b. storage tank
    c. style of painting
    d. type of timber
    e. fabric

36. Find a one-word anagram for PETES LAD.

37. Place two three-letter bits together to make a six-letter word.

    ICE MER RIN SAR SAL WHA PLA DIN LER MAN
    Clue: fish

38. Which of the following is not a boat?

    a. brougham
    b. frigate
    c. barque
    d. cutter
    e. dromond

39. What familiar phrase is represented below?

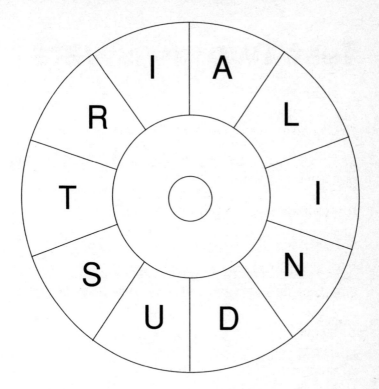

40. Fill in the blanks to find an eight-letter word.

_A_R_D_N

Test Two: Answers

1. 11.27 am; ie, 33 mins before 12 noon. $4 \times 33 = 132$ mins past 9 am = 11.12 am

2. Ban(glad)esh

3. boycott, proscribe

4. B; each horizontal line contains one each of the three different left-hand, right-hand and middle portions.

5. 1792 steps (896×2)

6. temper, ermine, negate

7. chaste/chased

8. D; the curved lines turn straight, and the straight lines turn curved.

9. astute

10. hesitate, relative

11. TY. Read along the top lines, middle lines and bottom lines in each set respectively to spell out the words: solitude, dedicate and alacrity.

12. $99; 4 + 5 = 9, 3 + 6 = 9$

13. February

14. kill two birds with one stone

15. card; all the words in list A can be prefixed with 'red', all the words in list B can be prefixed with 'blue'.

16. A; starting at the black circle the circles are in sets of five, which are being repeated, except that in each set of five the black circle moves up one space.

17. domains and aim; all the other words are in pairs so that each three-letter word is spelt backwards in the middle of one of the seven-letter words: precast/ace, panache/ can, attempt/met, sadness/end, special/ice, presume/use, suburbs/rub. The word *domains* spells iam backwards, not aim.

18. 3; starting at the top, and reading clockwise, each number, formed by the top and bottom digits in that order, is the previous number plus the sum of its digits.
    So, $12 + 1 + 2 = 15, 15 + 1 + 5 = 21$.

19. uniform

20. A; C and D are the same with black and white reversed, as are B and E.

21. c. a sail

22. d. a grist

23. a. a fish

24. desserts (or 'stressed' anti-clockwise)

25. beagle, barbet

26. 145. Each number is obtained by adding the previous four numbers.

27. C

28. d. steak

29. The most brilliantly dressed army will usually lose.

30. Each word has three letters in succession in the alphabet.

31. night

32. $(40; 4 \times 7 = 28) + (9 \times 2 = 18) = 46; (7 \times 3 = 21) + (8 \times 4 = 32) = 53; (5 \times 6 = 30) + (2 \times 5 = 10) = 40$

33. perishable

34. D

35. e. fabric

36. pedestal

37. plaice

38. a. brougham

39. industrial revolution

40. harridan

Test Three: Questions

1.

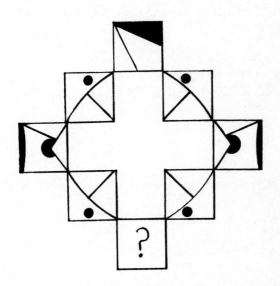

Which square below should replace the question mark?

A   B   C   D   E

2. What number should replace the question mark?

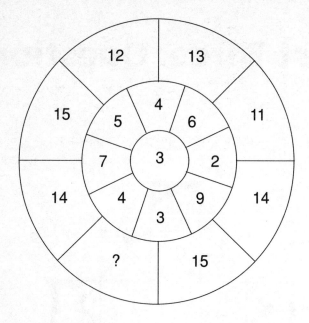

3. Which of the following is not an anagram of a type of dog?

    LOOPED
    NO SLAM
    BAG EEL
    SAIL UK
    BASTES

4. Consider the following list of words:

    mountain, wine, spoon, tennis

    Now choose just one of the following words which has something specific in common with them:

    Saturday, friendship, manners, hope, chant

5.

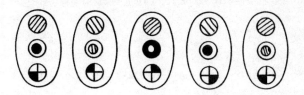

What comes next in the above sequence?

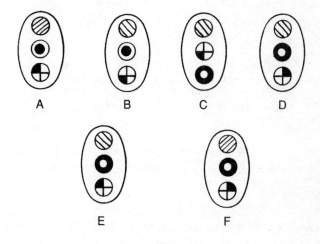

6. Find the starting point and track along the connecting lines from letter to letter to spell out a well-known phrase (4 2 4 5).

    Note: when travelling from letter to letter along a side of a triangle, lines may have to pass through letters that are not part of the solution.

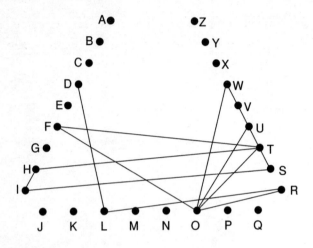

7. Which word, when inserted in the brackets, will complete the first word and start the second?

    high (   ) beat

8. Change one letter only from each word to form a well-known phrase.

    ail sands of neck

9. Which is the odd number out in each square?

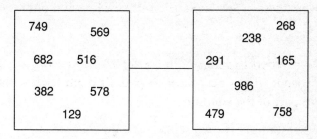

10. What three-letter word can be placed after each of the
    following to form five English words?

    F _ _ _
    H _ _ _
    P _ _ _
    CH _ _ _
    FL _ _ _

11.

  is to:

as

is to:

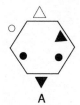   

   A   B   C   D

12. What is *meerschaum*?

    a. hard white mineral
    b. a prayer said at dawn
    c. a nerve-racking experience
    d. way of living
    e. a carved figure

13. What number should replace the question mark?

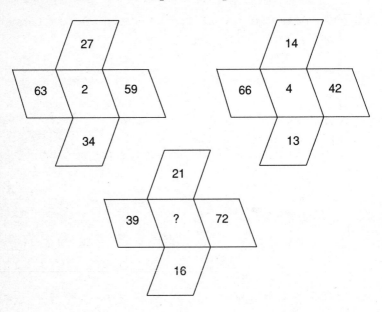

14.

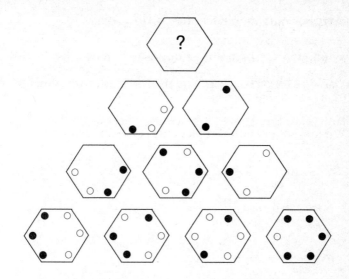

Which hexagon should replace the question mark?

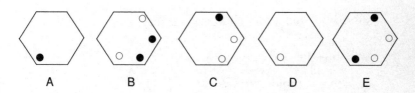

A   B   C   D   E

15. Insert the missing letters to find two words that form a phrase:

T O D C O D R C N T E

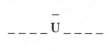

_ _ _ _ U _ _ _ _

–

Clue: harmonic excursion

16. Which two words are most alike in meaning?

    discipline, schism, blister, snatch, rift, signal

17. Which two words are most opposite in meaning?

    edacious, reserved, clean, rough, generous, anomalous

18. Which number should replace the question mark?

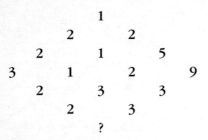

19. Mule is to slipper as sabot is to:

    shoe, boot, moccasin, sandal, clog.

20. Which is the odd one out?

    quick, curt, rapid, swift, fleet

21. What is the meaning of mantua?

    a. hat
    b. animal
    c. gown
    d. insect

22. What is the next number in this series?

    ½, ⅔, ⅞, 1⁵⁄₂₇, ?

23. What is the name given to a group of cranes (birds)?

    a. barren
    b. herd
    c. richesse
    d. stentation

24. Place two four-letter bits together to equal an eight-letter word.

    CONT PINE LLON BANT INUI EFFI CALA DINE TERA PAPI

25. What number should replace the question mark?

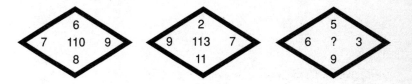

26. Fill in the letters to make two animals of six letters.

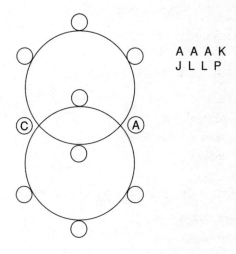

A A A K
J L L P

27.

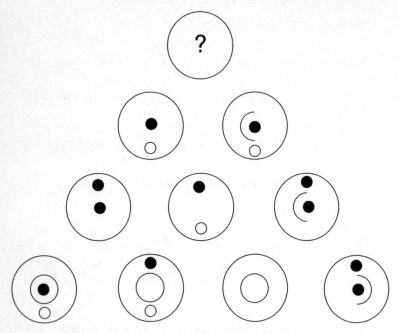

Which circle should replace the question mark?

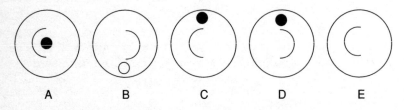

A   B   C   D   E

28. What is a hacienda?

   a. a plant
   b. a village
   c. a range of mountains
   d. a ranch
   e. a dance

29. All of the vowels have been removed from this trite saying by Judith Cohen. See if you can replace them.

    WLLMT LLJRH DHDCH S

30. What does nescient mean?

    a. agreeable
    b. hard of hearing
    c. ignorant
    d. hesitant

31. What is the next number in this series?

    ¼, ⅜, ⁹⁄₁₆, ²⁷⁄₃₂, 1¹⁷⁄₆₄, ?

32. Which circle cannot be made into a word?

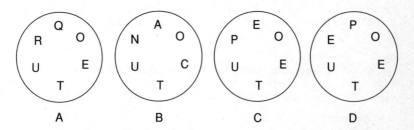

         A   B   C   D

33. Fill in the blanks and find two words that are synonyms.

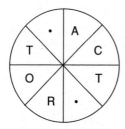 

34.

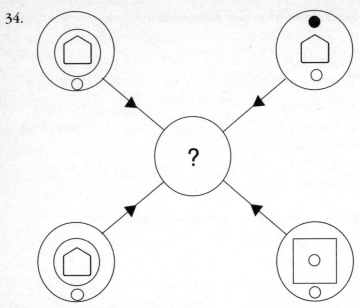

Each line and symbol that appears in the four outer circles, above, is transferred to the centre circle according to these rules. If a line or symbol occurs in the outer circles:

once:	it is transferred
twice:	it is possibly transferred
3 times:	it is transferred
4 times:	it is not transferred

Which of the circles A, B, C, D or E, shown below, should appear at the centre of the diagram, above?

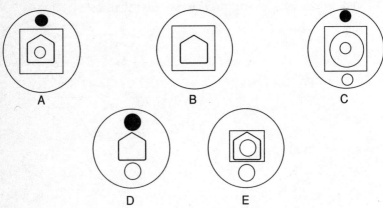

35. Replace the letters to make a word.

    _O_E_R_D

36. Which of the following is always part of frangipane?

    a. raspberries
    b. lemon
    c. cheese
    d. almonds
    e. melon

37. Which of the following is not a nautical term?

    a. RANIME
    b. CRANOH
    c. EBONAC
    d. YEHCOK
    e. YAPIRC

38. Find the number to replace the question mark.
    8, 10, 9¾, 8¼, 11½, 6½, ?

39. Find a 10-letter word by travelling from circle to circle.

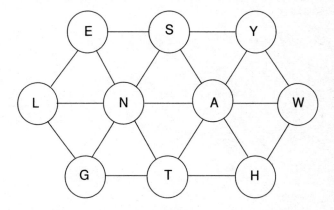

40. Find the longest word in the square by moving from letter to letter in any direction, but each letter must be used only once.

B	X	W	O	S
I	Q	U	R	K
C	T	E	J	N
P	V	H	M	L
F	A	G	D	Y

Test Three: Answers

1. A; directly opposite squares are a mirror image of each other.

2. 10; each number on the outside is the sum of the two numbers in the middle ring adjacent to it, plus the number in the centre. So, 4 + 3 + 3 = 10.

3. NO SLAM = salmon. The dogs are: looped = poodle; bag eel = beagle; sail UK = saluki; and bastes = basset.

4. manners; all words can be prefixed with *table*.

5. E; the sequence appears looking across each row of circles in the ellipses. The top row alternates right-sloping stripes, left-sloping stripes etc, the middle row is repeating the first three circles, and in the bottom row, the black segment is moving one segment clockwise at each stage.

6. out of this world

7. brow

8. all hands on deck

9. 569 and 986; all the others are in anagram pairs of numbers, 749/479, 682/268, 516/165, 382/238, 578/758 and 129/291.

10. air, to give fair, hair, pair, chair and flair.

11. D; the figures on the outside transfer to the inside and change shape and colour. So, a white circle on the outside becomes a black triangle on the inside.

12. a. a hard white mineral

13. 3; $39 + 72 = 111, 21 + 16 = 37, 111 \div 37 = 3$

14. D; the contents of each hexagon are determined by the contents of the two hexagons immediately below it. Where two identical circles appear in the same corner in these two hexagons, they are carried forward to the hexagon above but change from black to white and vice versa.

15. conducted tour

16. schism, rift

17. edacious, generous

18. 1; so that the total of each vertical line of numbers increases by one each time.

19. clog

20. curt

21. c. gown

22. $1\frac{47}{81}$ ($\times 1\frac{1}{3}$)

23. b. herd

24. papillon

25. 69; $(6 \times 9 = 54) + (7 \times 8 = 56) = 110$; $(2 \times 7 = 14) + (9 \times 11 = 99) = 113$; $(5 \times 3 = 15) + (6 \times 9 = 54) = 69$

26. jackal, alpaca

27. E. The symbols in the lower two circles combine to form the circle above, but similar symbols disappear.

28. d. a ranch

29. William Tell Jr had headaches

30. c. ignorant

31. $1\frac{115}{128}$ ($\times 1.5$)

32. D. The others are: a. torque, b. toucan, c. toupee

33. protract, lengthen

34. A

35. Lopeared

36. d. almonds

37. d. (hockey). The others are: marine, anchor, beacon, piracy.

38. 13¼. There are two series: + 1¾ and – 1¾: 8, 9¾, 11½, 13¼ and 10, 8¼, 6½.

39. lengthways

40. southernly

Test Four: Questions

1. How many circles on page 60 contain a black dot?

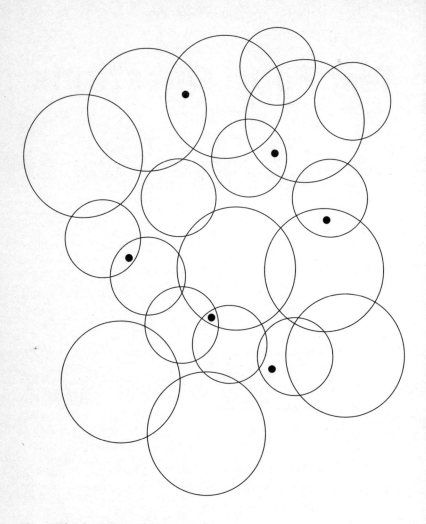

2. Which is the odd one out?

anther, flower, stigma, petal, nectar

3. Complete the bottom line of numbers.

7	4	9	2
11	16	9	13
22	20	24	25
?	?	?	?

4. Insert the word in brackets that means the same as the definitions outside the brackets.

    game bird (   ) cower

5. Which two rhyming words mean: fresh hint?

6.

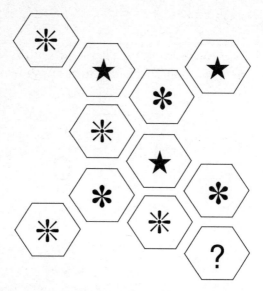

Which symbol should replace the question mark?

A   B   C

7.   Which of the following is not an anagram of the word:
ANAGRAMMATICALLY?

MANIACALLY TAG ARM
ILL MAY MAGNA CARTA
CLARITY AN AMALGAM
TINY MAGICAL ALARM
A MAGICAL MANLY ART
ARM MANLY GALACTICA
MY A CARNAL MAIL TAG
ARMY GALA CLAIMANT
ALARMING MALAY CAT

8. What number continues the following sequence?

   759, 675, 335, 165, ?

9. Find the starting point and read clockwise to find a familiar phrase (5 2 3 6). Only alternate letters are shown.

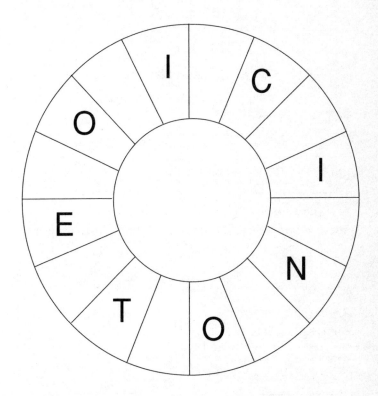

10. Which two words are most opposite in meaning?

    politician, principal, miscreant, subsidiary, practice, prosecutor

11.

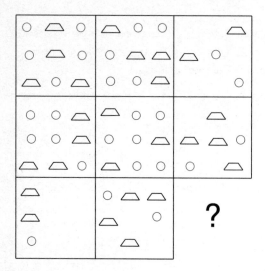

Which square below should replace the question mark?

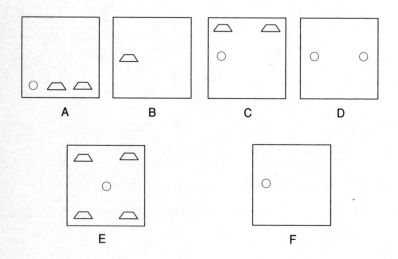

A   B   C   D

E   F

12. Complete the numbers in the final column.

15	20	19	20
14	23	9	?
5	15	24	?

13. Which word is the odd one out?

    auctioneers,   executioner,   postponed,   erroneously,
    weaponless

14. What numbers should replace the question marks?

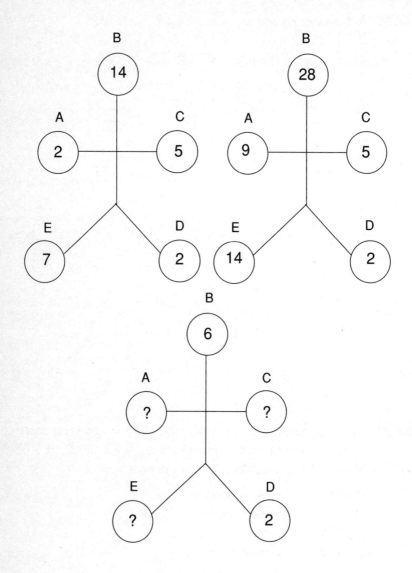

15. succeed is to prevail as fail is to:

contrive, agonize, destroy, founder, grovel

16. What letter should replace the question mark?

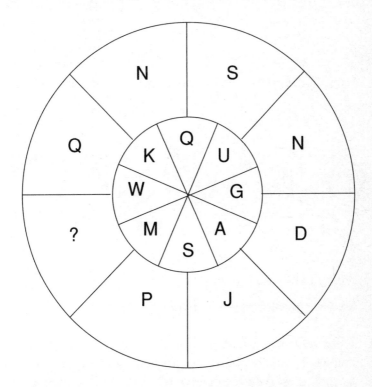

17. Solve the clues to find four six-letter words. The same three letters appear in each word, which are represented by XYZ below. XYZ is a familiar three-letter word.

XYZ_ _ _   most venerable
XYZ _   turned over
_ _XYZ_   defend
_ _ XYZ_   castigates

18.

What comes next in the above sequence?

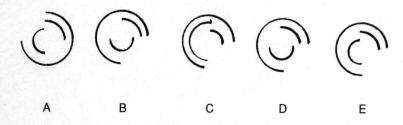

A   B   C   D   E

19. Which two words are most alike in meaning?

waspish, jovial, peppery, prudent, perilous, lewd

20. A car travels the first half of a motorway journey at an average speed of 40 mph, and the second half of the journey at an average speed of 60 mph. What is the average speed for the entire journey?

21. What is the name given to a group of trout?

    a. collection
    b. plump
    c. glean
    d. hover

22. Place two three-letter bits together to make a six-letter word.

    GER BOL EPR GER TLY BAL SHE BAD CAT TIG

    Clue: animal

23. What is the meaning of kibble?

    a. iron bucket
    b. card game
    c. a quarrel
    d. fruit

24. Which is the odd one out?

    midge
    bassoon
    solemn
    dabbled
    brilliant
    coding
    carpet

25. Fill in the letters to make two birds of six letters.

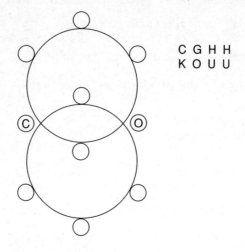

C G H H
K O U U

26. What familiar phrase is suggested below?

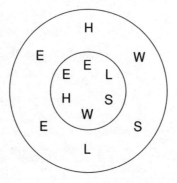

27. Each of the nine squares in the grid marked 1A to 3C should incorporate all the lines and symbols that are shown in the squares of the same letter and number immediately above and to the left. For example, 2B should incorporate all the lines and symbols that are in 2 and B.

One of the squares is incorrect. Which one is it?

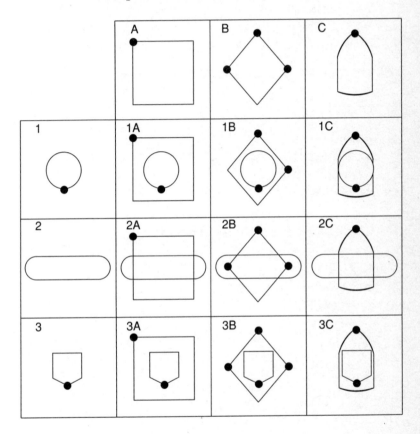

28. Which four-letter word can be placed in front of all of these words to make new words?

   _ _ _ _ BAKED
   _ _ _ _ BOILED
   _ _ _ _ BOARD
   _ _ _ _ BACK
   _ _ _ _ HEADED

29. Fill in the missing vowels to make a trite saying.

   THDMM RTHLG HTTHG RTRTH SCNDL

30. What is a jacana?

   a. bird
   b. fish
   c. insect
   d. animal

31. Which of the following is not a bird?

   a. TCTALE
   b. RYCANA
   c. NIRMEL
   d. FIFPUN
   e. ETIPEW

32. What number should replace the question mark?

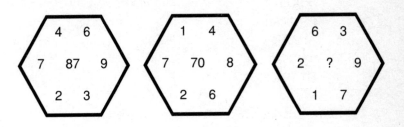

33. Find the missing letters to make a word.

34.

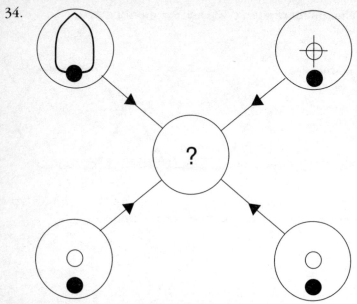

Each line and symbol that appears in the four outer circles, above, is transferred to the centre circle according to these rules. If a line or symbol occurs in the outer circles:

once: it is transferred
twice: it is possibly transferred
3 times: it is transferred
4 times: it is not transferred

Which of the circles A, B, C, D or E shown below should appear at the centre of the diagram, above?

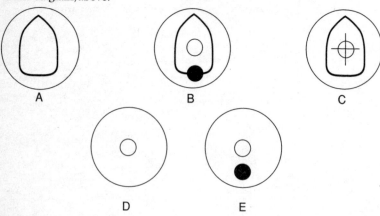

35. What do these words have in common?

    a. alone
    b. hold
    c. anger
    d. mask
    e. force

36. Find a one-word anagram for PAUL RICE.

37. Place two four-letter bits together to equal an eight-letter word.

    COCH, MAND, GERM, TONS, HLEA, LOCY, FRAC, TROC, ITES, IDIO

38. What have these words in common?

    cashed
    helmet
    soaking
    sublime
    plummet

39. Fill in the blanks to find two words that are antonyms.

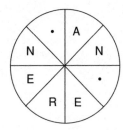 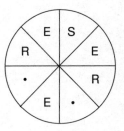

40. Since my birth I have had a birthday cake with candles, one
     for each year of my birthday, each year.

To date, I have had 325 candles. How old am I?

Test Four: Answers

1. 12

2. flower; this is the whole thing, the rest are parts of a flower.

3. 49, 46, 47, 44. Look at pairs of lines: 7 + 9 = 16, 4 + 9 = 13, 9 + 2 = 11, 7 + 2 = 9. Therefore, 22 + 24 = 46, 20 + 24 = 44, 24 + 25 = 49, 22 + 25 = 47.

4. quail

5. new clue

6. C; so that each straight line of three hexagons contains one each of the three different symbols.

7. tiny magical alarm

8. 80; each number is formed by multiplying the number formed by the first two digits of the previous number by its third digit. So, 16 × 5 = 80.

9. signs of the zodiac

10. principal, subsidiary

11. F; the contents of the last square in each row and column is determined by the contents of the first two squares. Only when the same figure appears in the same position is a figure carried forward to the final square, in which case two circles become a trapezium, and two trapeziums become a circle.

12. 5 and 14; each number represents a letter of the alphabet according to its numerical position in the alphabet. The letters in each column spell out three letter numbers: 1, 2, 6 and 10.

13. weaponless; all the other words contain the adjacent letters ONE.

14.

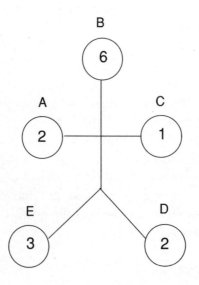

In each figure, A + C = E, A + C + E = B, B/E = D.

15. founder

16. R; the letter on the outside is positioned midway between its two adjacent letters on the inside, in the alphabet.

17. XYZ = OLD: oldest, folded, uphold, scolds

18. B; the outer arc moves 90° clockwise at each stage, the middle arc moves 180° at each stage, the inner arc moves 180° at each stage.

19. waspish, peppery

20. 48mph. Say the journey takes 120 miles. The first half of the journey (60 miles) takes 60/40 = 1.5 hours; the second half takes 60/60 = 1.0 hour. So, the journey of 120 miles takes 1.5 + 1.0 = 2.5 hours and therefore, the average speed is 120/2.5 = 48mph.

21. d. hover

22. badger

23. a. iron bucket

24. midge, the others start with a fish: bass, sole, dab, brill, cod, carp.

25. cuckoo, chough

26. wheels within wheels

27. IB

28. hard

29. The dimmer the light the greater the scandal.

30. a. bird

31. a. tctale = cattle. The others are: canary, merlin, puffin, peewit.

32. 63. Multiply opposites:

$4 \times 3 = 12$	$1 \times 6 = 6$	$6 \times 7 = 42$
$2 \times 6 = 12$	$2 \times 4 = 8$	$1 \times 3 = 3$
$7 \times 9 = 63$	$7 \times 8 = 56$	$2 \times 9 = 18$
Total: 87	70	63

33. eggplant

34. C

35. Two letters can be placed at the beginning to make a new word: abalone, behold, changer, damask, enforce.

36. peculiar

37. trochlea

38. They all contain the name of a tree: ash, elm, oak, lime, plum.

39. endanger, reserved

40. 25

Test Five: Questions

1. A statue is being carved by a sculptor. The original piece of marble weighed 250kg. In the first week 30 per cent is cut away. In the second week 20 per cent of the remainder is cut away. In the third week the statue is completed when 25 per cent of the remainder is cut away. What is the weight of the final statue?

2. Which word in brackets is closest in meaning to the word in capitals?

   ESPOUSAL (advocacy, suspicion, agreement, bias, honesty)

3. Which is the odd one out?

   relating
   triangle
   rambling
   integral
   altering

4.   Which is the odd one out?

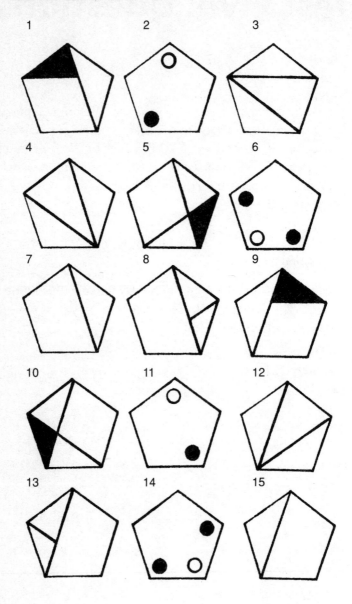

5. Which number is the odd one out?

   159
   248
   963
   357
   951
   852

6. Sunday
   Monday
   Tuesday
   Wednesday
   Thursday
   Friday
   Saturday

   What day is two days before the day immediately following the day three days before the day two days after the day immediately before Friday?

7.

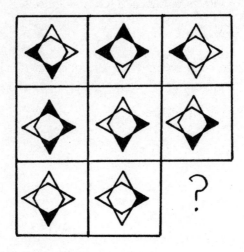

Which square should replace the question mark?

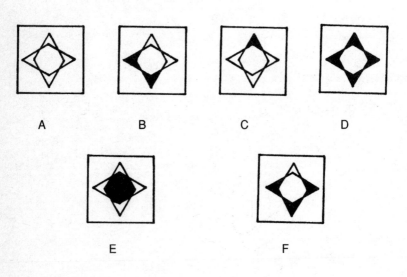

8. What is the longest English word that can be created from this set of letters, using each letter once only?

   NUHRIAKMTE

9. Apart from each having five letters, what do these words have in common?

   groom, spank, plaid, breve

10. Which is the odd one out?

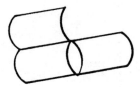

A

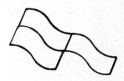

B

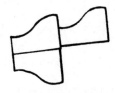

C

D

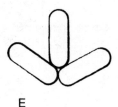

E

11. What four-digit number should replace the question mark?

    4342 (3176) 1726
    7995 (7516) 2162
    8418 (? ? ? ?) 1725

12. hypotenuse is to triangle as chord is to:

    polygon, cone, rhomboid, circle, heptagon

13. Insert the name of a type of fruit into the bottom line to complete nine three-letter words reading downwards.

A	S	P	C	R	O	F	M	C
R	I	E	A	U	D	O	A	O
–	–	–	–	–	–	–	–	–

14. Start at a corner letter and spiral clockwise round the perimeter, finishing at the centre letter, to spell out a nine-letter word. You have to provide the missing letters.

S		E
E	_	R
D	D	A

    (first row: S, _, E)

15. If meat in a river (3 in 6) is T(ham)es, can you find a word meaning *reconstitute* in the title of a Shakespeare play (6 in 7 3 7)?

16. Change one letter only from each word to form a well-known phrase.

    WE AIL ANY AND ILL

17. Find two eight-letter words, one reading clockwise round the inner circle, and the other reading anti-clockwise round the outer circle, that are opposite in meaning. You have to provide the missing letters.

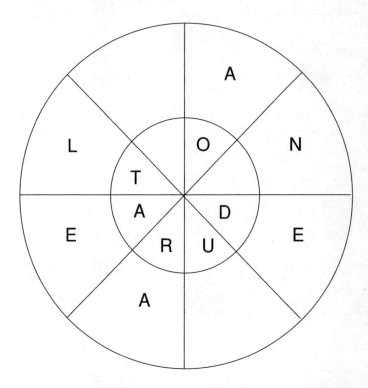

18.

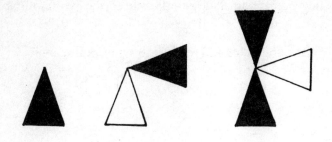

What continues the above sequence?

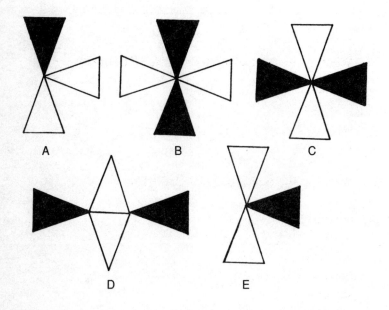

19. Use every letter of the newspaper headline below, once each only, to spell out three kinds of fish.

    Nomad Robs Camel

20. What number should replace the question marks?

    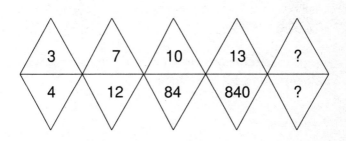

21. What is the name given to a group of hounds?

    a. mute
    b. sedge
    c. watch
    d. clutter

22. Which is the odd one out in this list?

    tackled
    scarlet
    grammar
    godetia
    stacking
    starving

23. What is the next number in this sequence?

    $\frac{7}{8}, -\frac{7}{24}, \frac{7}{72}, -\frac{7}{216}$?

24. What is a pumpion?

    a. drink
    b. pumpkin
    c. carriage
    d. type of cheese

25. Find a 10-letter word moving from circle to circle. Each circle must only be used once.

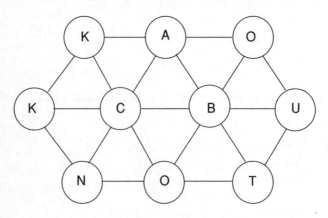

26.

EVERY	AND	IS	HILL
AGAINST	NO	WHICH	THE
WAY	ALWAYS	LUCK	TIME
YOU	BAD	JUST	RIDE
WIND	UP	MATTER	ITS

Try to re-arrange the above into a trite saying.

27.

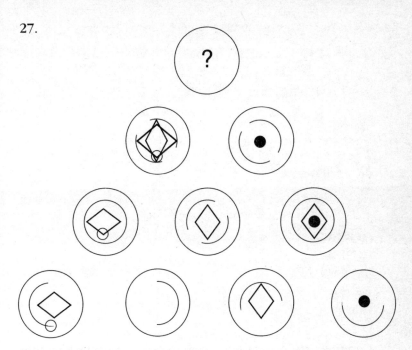

Which circle should replace the question mark?

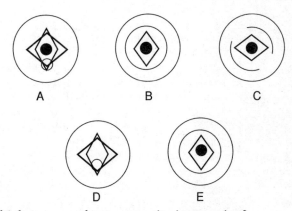

A   B   C

D   E

28. Which two words are opposite in meaning?

severity, caution, incite, calm, impulse, wonder, stand, dismiss

29. Fill in the missing vowels to make a trite saying.

    FLSRS HNWHR FLSHV BNBFR

30. What is the meaning of epopee?

    a. epic poem
    b. weapon
    c. eye glass
    d. small beard

31. Which of the following is not a tree?

    LIOWWL
    CUPESR
    VATRAC
    CICAAA
    DODERA

32. Complete the words that are synonyms, clockwise or anti-clockwise.

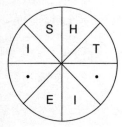
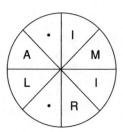

33. Find the missing letters to make a word.

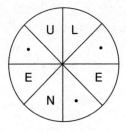

34.

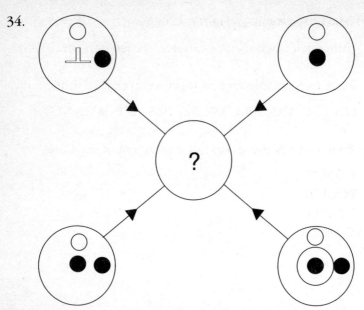

Each line and symbol that appears in the four outer circles, above, is transferred to the centre circle according to these rules. If a line or symbol occurs in the outer circles:

once:	it is transferred
twice:	it is possibly transferred
3 times:	it is transferred
4 times:	it is not transferred

Which of the circles, A, B, C, D or E shown below should appear at the centre of the diagram, above?

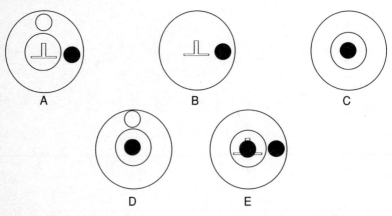

35. Which two words mean the same?

    bathos, spectacles, junta, carriage, archetype, cabal

36. Place two three-letter bits together to equal a drink.

    SES, SQU, CAS, ARR, AST, SIS, POS, ACE, WHI, NDY

37. Which one of these was not a president of the USA?

    RACRET
    ROOVHE
    PINCHAL
    TAMRUN
    SLIWNO

38. Which is the odd one out?

    bazooka, shrapnel, claymore, harpoon, bonanza, arquebus

39. Fill in the blanks to find two words that are antonyms.

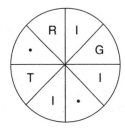 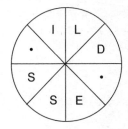

40. What number should replace the question mark?

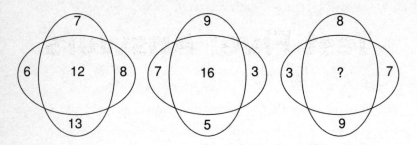

Test Five: Answers

1. 105kg; $250 \times 0.7 \times 0.8 \times 0.75$

2. advocacy

3. rambling; the rest are all anagrams of each other.

4. 3; the rest all have a mirror image pair, 1/9, 2/11, 4/12, 5/10, 6/14, 7/15, 8/13

5. 248; in the rest there is the same difference between each digit, eg, 8 (-3) 5 (-3) 2.

6. Tuesday

7. A; black segments only appear in the final square in each row and column when they appear in the same position in the first two squares.

8. ruminate

9. Their last four letters spell out another word reading backwards; groom/moor, spank/knap, plaid/dial, breve/ever.

10. C; it contains one figure which has been inverted and cannot be rotated to look the same.

11. 4725; delete the digits outside the brackets that appear twice, and insert the remaining digits in the brackets in the same order that they appear outside the brackets – *8418* (4725) *1725*.

12. circle

13. cranberry, to give arc, sir, pea, can, rub, ode, for, mar, coy.

14. desperado

15. Measu(re For M)easure

16. be all and end all.

17. obdurate, amenable

18. C; each triangle changes from black to white in turn. At each stage a new triangle is added moving anti-clockwise, and this new triangle first of all appears black, then alternates black/white at each stage.

19. bream, cod, salmon

20. 16 at the top, 10920 at the bottom.

    The top number is the sum of all the digits in the previous diamond (1 + 3 + 8 + 4 + 0). The bottom number is the product of the two numbers in the previous diamond (13 × 840).

21. a. mute

22. scarlet; the other words all carry an animal in reverse: elk, ram, dog, cat, rat.

23. $\frac{7}{48}$ (x − ⅓)

24. b. pumpkin

25. knockabout

26. No matter which way you ride, it is always up hill and against the wind every time, just bad luck.

27. A; the two circles below combine to produce the circle above, but similar symbols disappear.

28. Incite, calm

29. Fools rush in where fools have been before.

30. epic poem

31. Vatrac (cravat). The others are: willow, spruce, acacia, deodar.

32. Thievish, criminal

33. Julienne

34. e

35. cabal, junta

36. cassis

37. Chaplin. The others are: Carter, Hoover, Truman, Wilson.

38. bonanza

39. mildness, rigidity

40. 4; (13 – 7 = 6) × (8 – 6 = 2) = 12; (9 – 5 = 4) × (7 – 3 = 4) = 16; (9 – 8 = 1) × (7 – 3 = 4) = 4

Test Six: Questions

1. Which is the odd one out?

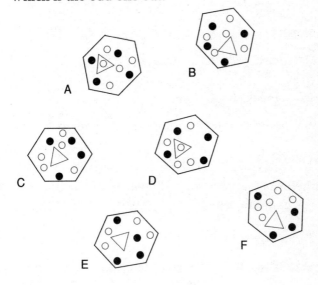

2. By starting at the Q in the centre and moving from letter to adjacent letter to an outside Z, how many different ways can the word QUIZ be spelt out?

```
            Z
         Z  I  Z
      Z  I  U  I  Z
   Z  I  U  Q  U  I  Z
      Z  I  U  I  Z
         Z  I  Z
            Z
```

3. pediform is to foot as reniform is to:

   heart, kidney, tooth, beak, fingers

4. Which is the odd one out?

   pentad, limerick, quatrain, quincunx, pentagon

5. MOOD SLEEP

   The above is an anagram of which two words that are similar in meaning?

   Clue: sit still.

6. What letter should replace the question mark?

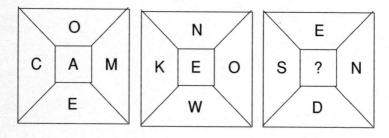

7. How many lines appear below?

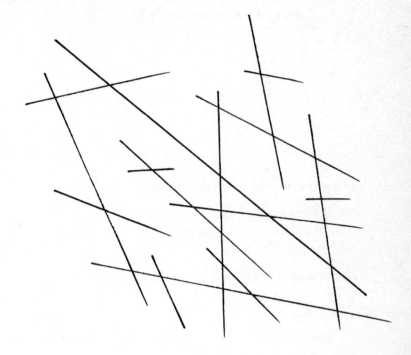

8. What is the length of line AB? (NB: Not to scale.)

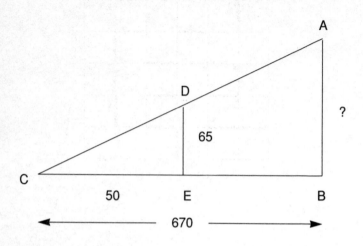

9. Complete the names of three animals by inserting the missing letters:

_ A _ G _ R
_ O _ K _ Y
_ A _ B _ T

Now rearrange the nine missing letters to find two words (6, 3) in answer to the clue: *greased palms.*

10. Insert the following words into the grid opposite:

XENON	HOAX	PEA
ONION	HOLE	EWE
NINJA		DIG
NEWEL		SHY
LAUGH		DEW
SALON		OWE

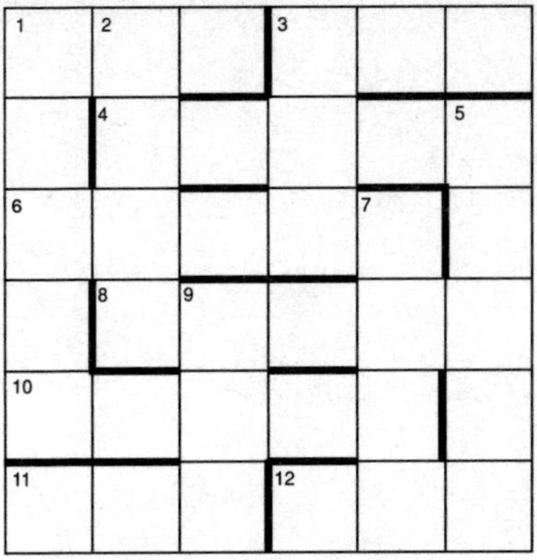
1
2
3
4
5
6
7
8
9
10
11
12

11.

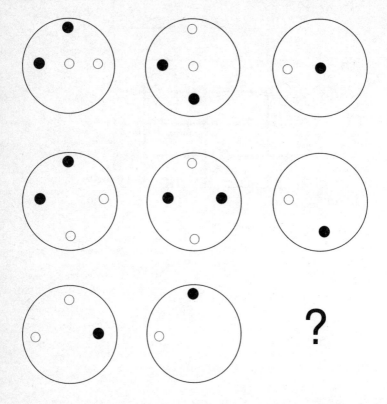

What circle should replace the question mark?

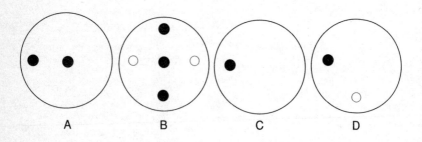

12. What number should replace the question mark?

15	2	7	10
7	8	3	4
21	6	11	16
13	4	7	?

13. Which two rhyming words solve the following clue?

    Sylvan flower seller

14. Which of the following is not an anagram of a type of ship?

    ARK NET
    LAY LEG
    NUCHAL
    BE TASK
    SPA MAN

15. Find the starting point and track along the connecting lines from letter to letter to spell out a well-known phrase (6 2 6).

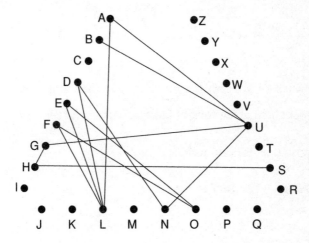

16.

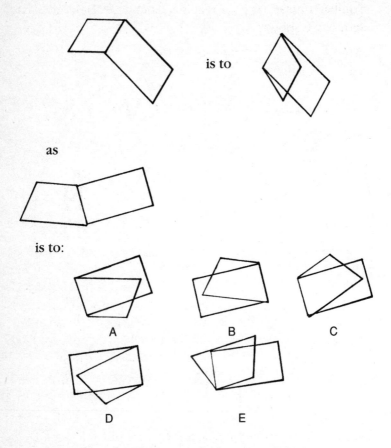

is to

as

is to:

A B C

D E

17. Which two words are most alike in meaning?

speech, hearsay, fury, boast, rumour, extract

18. Which is the odd number out?

9421, 7532, 9854, 8612, 6531, 8541

19. Find the starting point and fill in the blanks to find a familiar phrase (6 5 4) reading clockwise. Only alternate letters are shown.

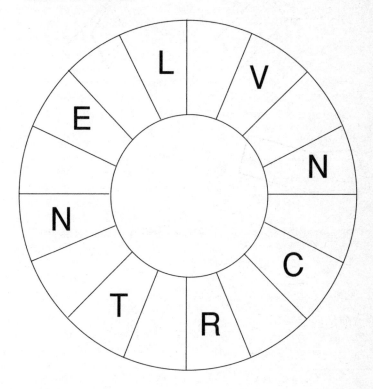

20. Change one letter only from each word to spell out a well-known phrase.

    ACE FOUR ACE

21. What is the name for a group of otters?

    a. gang
    b. bevy
    c. sloth
    d. tiding

22. Which five-letter word can be placed in front of each of these words to make new words?

    _ _ _ _ _ RUNNER
    _ _ _ _ _ AGE
    _ _ _ _ _ LINE
    _ _ _ _ _ RANK
    _ _ _ _ _ MAN

23. What is a gridelin?

    a. colour
    b. cooking utensil
    c. cover over sewer
    d. railway sleeper

24. Place two three-letter bits together to equal an animal.

    ONE, POL, VIC, ERA, BIS, UNA

25. Which circle cannot be made into a word?

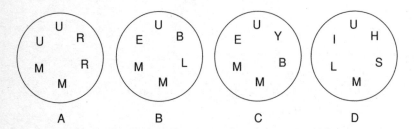

26. Fill in the blanks to find two words that are antonyms.

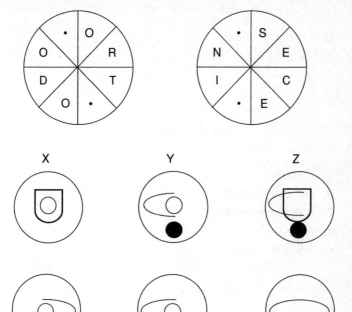

27.

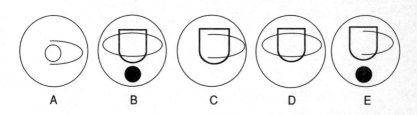

Which symbol should replace the question mark?

A   B   C   D   E

28. Which is the odd one out?

    timer
    loots
    repel
    times
    spots

29. Find a one-word anagram for SHOT PILL.

30. What is a plie?

    a. a climbing tool
    b. a ballet movement
    c. a pie
    d. a fencing stroke

31. What are the next two letters in this sequence?

    A, F, H, K, N, ?, ?

32. Fill in the blanks to find an eight-letter word.

33. Fill in the blanks and find two words that are synonyms.

34.

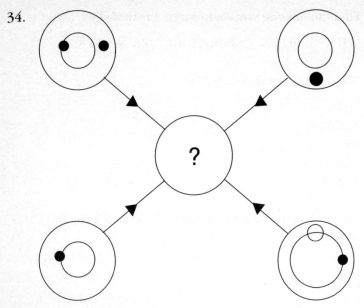

Each line and symbol that appears in the four outer circles, above, is transferred to the centre circle according to these rules. If a line or symbol occurs in the outer circles:

once: it is transferred
twice: it is possibly transferred
3 times: it is transferred
4 times: it is not transferred

Which of the circles A, B, C, D or E shown below should appear at the centre of the diagram, above?

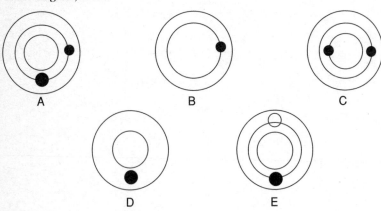

35. Find the missing vowels to make a trite saying.

    WHNTH BLLRN GSTHR HDBTT RBSMS PPR

36. Which of these is not an island?

    LICSLY
    NAGPEN
    KENROY
    DOLNON
    YANMAC

37. Find a six-letter word using only these four letters: A, K, L, I.

38. Place two four-letter bits together to make an eight-letter word.

    RONI, DAMA, TION, RENI, POEN, PENT, AGOS, MACA, GADE, TICS

39. What number should replace the question mark?

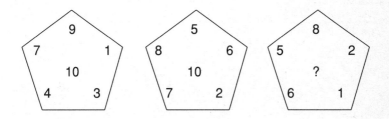

40. Find a 10-letter word by moving from circle to circle but you may only use each circle once.

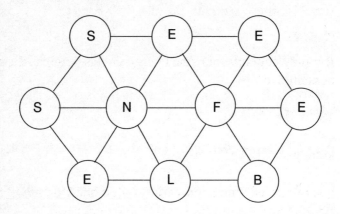

Test Six: Answers

1. E; it only contains four small white circles whereas the rest contain five.

2. 28

3. kidney

4. quatrain; it is connected with the number four, whilst the rest all have a connection with the number five.

5. pose, model

6. T; the letters in the middle convert the verb around the outside into past tense: come/came, know/knew, send/sent.

7. 16

8. 871; 65/50 × 670

9. badger, monkey, rabbit. The missing letters can be arranged to spell out *bribed men*.

10.

¹S	²H	Y	³D	E	W
A	⁴O	N	I	O	⁵N
⁶L	A	U	G	⁷H	I
O	⁸X	⁹E	N	O	N
¹⁰N	E	W	E	L	J
¹¹O	W	E	¹²P	E	A

11. C; the contents of the third circle in each row and column is determined by the contents of the previous two circles. Only when black or white dots appear in the same position in each of these two circles are they carried forward to the third circle, but then change from black to white and vice versa.

12. 10; in each row and column the difference between alternate digits is the same, ie, $16 - 10 = 10 - 4$.

13. forest florist

14. BE TASK = basket; the ships are, in order: tanker, galley, launch, sampan.

15. bundle of laughs

16. C; the left-hand portion is folded over onto the right-hand portion.

17. hearsay, rumour

18. 8612; all the other numbers have their digits in descending order.

19. tender loving care

20. act your age

21. b. bevy

22. front

23. a. colour

24. vicuna

25. C. A is murmur; B is mumble; D is mulish.

26. orthodox, seceding

27. E; x is added to y to make z; 1 is added to 2 to make 3, but like symbols disappear.

28. times; the other words also make words when spelt backwards.

29. hilltops

30. b. a ballet movement

31. Y, Z; the letters made with three straight lines.

32. yashmaks

33. immodest, indecent

34. E

35. When the bell rings there had better be some supper.

36. London. The others are: Scilly, Penang, Orkney, Cayman.

37. alkali

38. macaroni

39. 8; (9 + 7 + 1 = 17) – (4 + 3 = 7) = 10; (8 + 5 + 6 = 19) – (7 + 2 = 9) = 10; (5 + 8 + 2 = 15) – (6 + 1 = 7) = 8

40. feebleness

Test Seven: Questions

1. Which of the circles, A, B, C, D, E or F, should replace the question mark in the bottom large circle?

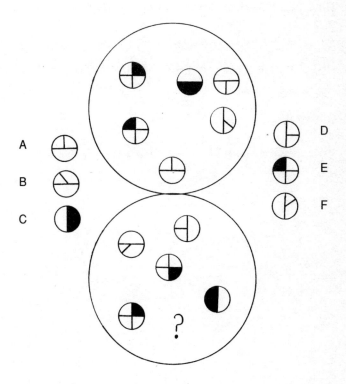

2. Change SEEK to FIND in three links by changing one letter at a time.

    SEEK

    _ _ _ _

    _ _ _ _

    _ _ _ _

    FIND

3. Six synonyms of the keyword SKILFUL are given. Take one letter in turn from each of these synonyms to spell out a further synonym of SKILFUL:

    able, adept, dextrous, proficient, accomplished, competent

4. MUTINY (MILKY) MEEKLY

    Using the same rules as above, what word is coded to go in the brackets below?

    ALIGHT (_ _ _ _ _) BONNET

5. What number should replace the question mark?

    ```
                    7
              5           9
         8         8           4
      10        3        10         7
    1        ?        8         3         11
    ```

6.   What letter should replace the question mark?

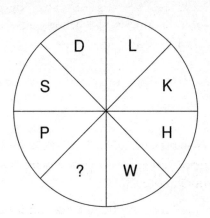

7.

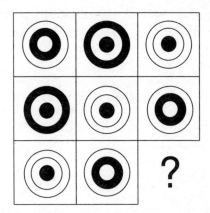

Which square should replace the question mark?

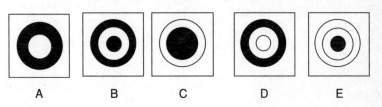

8. At a recent election, a total of 93,648 votes were cast for the four candidates, the winner exceeding his opponents by 25,627, 10,681 and 5,924 votes respectively. How many votes were cast for each candidate?

9. Which two letters come next in the following sequence?

   A, D, I, P, Y, CF, DI, FD, ?

10. Insert the missing word:

    DART   (STRANDED)   SEND
    DINE   (DILIGENT)   ?

11. A B C D E F G H

    What letter is two to the right of the letter immediately to the right of the letter two to the left of the letter three to the right of the letter immediately to the left of the letter E?

12.

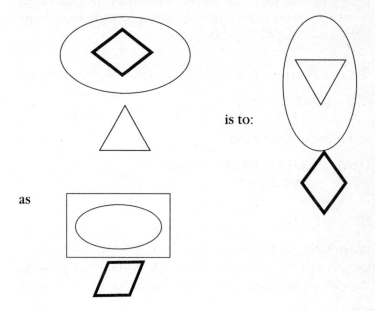

is to:

as

is to:

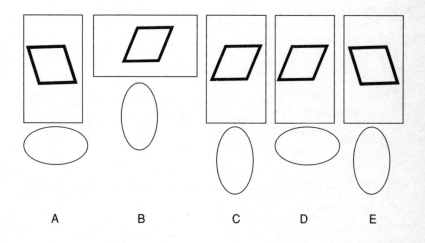

A   B   C   D   E

13. Insert the word in brackets that means the same as the definitions outside the brackets.

    circuit (   ) splash

14. What number should replace the question mark?

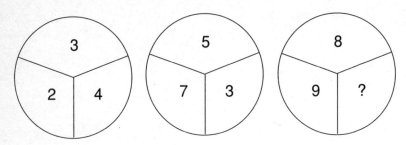

15. Find the starting point and track from letter to adjacent letter horizontally and vertically, but not diagonally, to spell out a 12-letter word. You have to provide the missing letters.

	E	E	
T	_	I	P
A	L	R	E

16. What is the meaning of plenary?

    a. easy to bend
    b. overabundance
    c. able to absorb
    d. open to all
    e. acceptable

17. Change one letter only from each word to form a well-known phrase.

    TO LIVE NOT MAKES

18. Which two words are most alike in meaning?

    accommodate, bilk, score, chat, swindle, wind

19. What number should replace the question mark?

4	7	3	8	9	2
?	9	0	2	5	1
5	1	6	3	5	9

20.

What comes next in the above sequence?

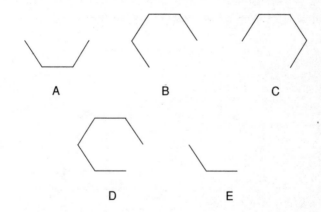

A   B   C

D   E

21. Which of the following is not clothing?

    a. togue
    b. hassock
    c. cassock
    d. chapeau

22. Fill in the missing vowels to find a trite saying.

    CLTTRD DSKMN FGNS

23. What is a picot?

    a. sword fish
    b. jewellery
    c. fabric
    d. loop of thread

24. What is the name of a group of badgers?

    a. volery
    b. trip
    c. covert
    d. sett

25. What familiar phrase is represented below?

```
        PORTTAXUGAL
```

26. Find the missing letters to make a word.

27. Each of the nine squares in the grid marked 1A to 3C should incorporate all the lines and symbols that are shown in the squares of the same letter and number immediately above and to the left. For example, 2B should incorporate all the lines and symbols that are in 2 and B.

    One of the squares is incorrect. Which one is it?

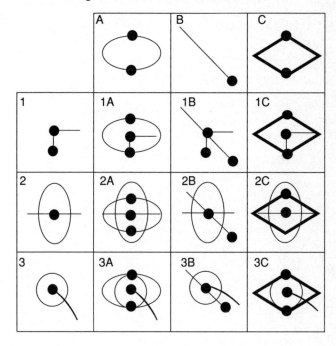

28. Solve the anagram to find a one-word answer:
    HEED LARKS.

29. Replace the missing vowels to make a word: SPGNLT.

30. Find a six-letter word using only these four letters:
    L I W O.

31. Find the number to replace the question mark.

    0.67, 0.69, 0.48, 0.88, 0.29, 1.07, ?

32. Find the 10-letter word:

    _A_A_R_P_S

33. Fill in the blanks to find two words that are synonyms.

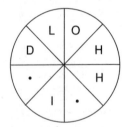

34.

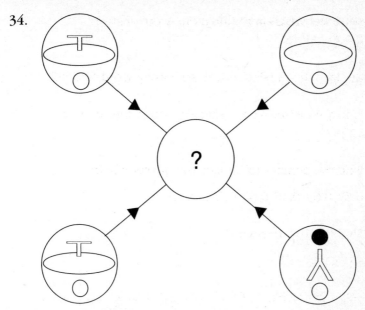

Each line and symbol that appears in the four outer circles, above, is transferred to the centre circle according to these rules. If a line or symbol occurs in the outer circles:

once: it is transferred
twice: it is possibly transferred
3 times: it is transferred
4 times: it is not transferred

Which of the circles A, B, C, D or E, shown below, should appear at the centre of the diagram, above?

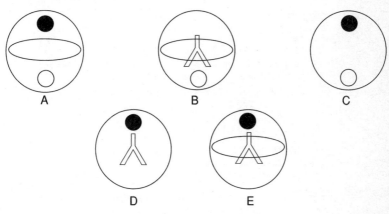

131

35. What activity is langlauf?

    a. boating
    b. fishing
    c. skating
    d. skiing

36. What is the name given to a group of trees?

    a. bulk
    b. bundle
    c. stand
    d. branch
    e. standard

37. What is drugget?

    a. a cart
    b. fabric
    c. bridge
    d. haberdashers

38. What is the name given to a group of foxes?

    a. a skein
    b. a slink
    c. a clamour
    d. an earth

39. Move in any direction to find a 10-letter word; each letter must only be used once.

B	X	Q	L	G
I	Y	U	V	J
M	S	W	D	T
E	C	R	F	H
N	P	A	K	D

40. What number should replace the question mark?

```
    6  2              8  1              7  9
  3 16  9           2 15  4           1  ?  6
    7  1              9  3              7  3
```

Test Seven: Answers

1. D; each circle in the bottom half is a repeat of a circle in the top half, but rotated 90° clockwise.

2. SEEK
    SEED
    FEED
    FEND
    FIND

    Some variations are possible and allowable.

3. adroit

4. agent:

    A L I G H T (A G E N T) B O N N E T
    1   2   5   1 2 3 4 5   4 3

5. 10; starting from the bottom and working to the top, each triangular group of three numbers totals 21.

6. O; opposite letters are the same number of letters from the beginning and end of the alphabet respectively.

7. B; so that each row and column contains one each of the three different symbols.

8. The number of votes received by the winning candidate was (93648 + 25627 + 10681 + 5924) divided by 4 = 33970.

   $$\begin{array}{lr}
    & 33970 \\
   \text{The second received } 33970 - 5924 = & 28046 \\
   \text{The third received } 33970 - 10681 = & 23289 \\
   \text{The fourth received } 33970 - 25627 = & \underline{8343} \\
   \text{Total} & 93648
   \end{array}$$

9. HA; take the numerical position of each letter in the alphabet to reveal the sequence of consecutive square numbers 1, 4, 9, 16, 25, 36, 49, 64, 81.

10. gilt; *dart*, *send* is an anagram of *stranded*; *dine*, *gilt* is an anagram of *diligent*.

11. H

12. E. The rectangle rotates 90°, the parallelogram flips over and goes inside the rectangle and the ellipse rotates 90° and goes below the rectangle.

13. lap

14. 7; add the numbers in the same segments of the first two circles to obtain the numbers in the same segments in the third circle. So, 3 + 5 = 8, 2 + 7 = 9, 4 + 3 = 7.

15. experimental; add the letters e, m and n.

16. d. open to all

17. go like hot cakes

18. bilk, swindle

19. 9; add the top line of numbers to the bottom line to obtain the middle line, ie: 473892 + 516359 = 990251.

20. B; there are two alternate sequences. In the first, the hexagon is losing one side at a time, in the other the hexagon is being constructed one line at a time.

21. b. hassock

22. A cluttered desk a man of genius.

23. d. loop of thread

24. d. sett

25. Inland Revenue

26. knothole

27. 2C

28. sheldrake

29. espagnolette

30. willow

31. 0.10.There are two series: – 0.19 and + 0.19:

    (–0 19)   0.67, 0.48, 0.29, 0.10
    (+ 0.19)   0.69, 0.88, 1.07, 1.26

32. paragraphs

33. restrain, withhold

34. E

35. d. skiing

36. c. stand

37. b. fabric

38. d. an earth

39. housecraft

40. 11. Opposite numbers are deducted then added:

6 – 1 = 5	8 – 3 = 5	7 – 3 = 4
7 – 2 = 5	4 – 2 = 2	9 – 7 = 2
9 – 3 = 6 +	9 – 1 = 8 +	6 – 1 = 5 +
16	15	11

Test Eight: Questions

1.

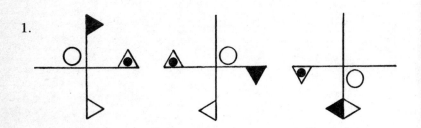

Which option continues the above sequence?

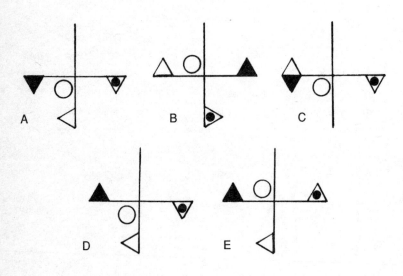

2. A bag of potatoes weighs 16 kg divided by a quarter of its weight. How much does the bag weigh?

3. Rift is to valley as mesa is to:

    desert, mountain, plain, hill, highland

4. Which two words are most opposite in meaning?

    inbound, intricate, erratic, warm, simple, fertile

5. Transfer the squares into the blank grid in such a way that a two-letter word is formed by each pair of adjoining letters and a 12-letter word is formed reading clockwise around the outside perimeter.

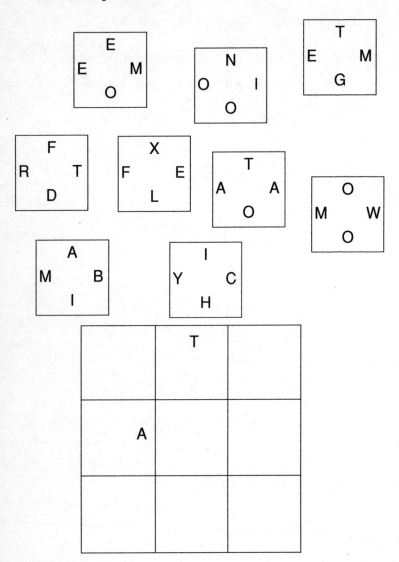

6.   Which is the odd one out?

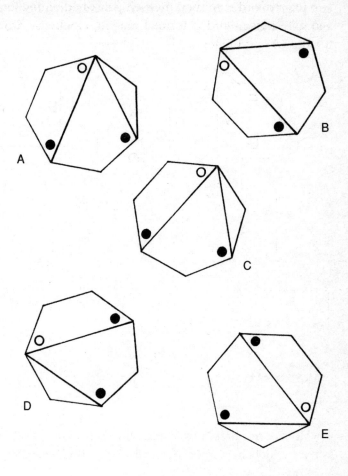

7. If planet A takes two years to revolve once round its sun, and planet B takes one year, when will they next both be in line with the sun?

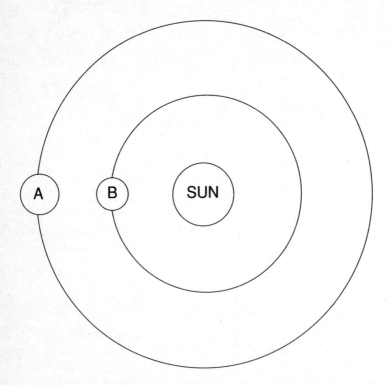

8. A well-known phrase has been divided into groups of three letters, which have then been placed in the wrong order. Find the phrase:

EBU EHO ETH LLB RNS TAK YTH

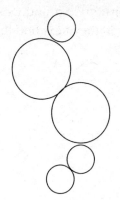

is to:

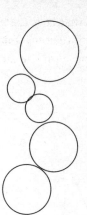

as

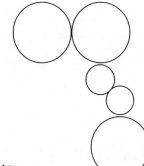

is to:

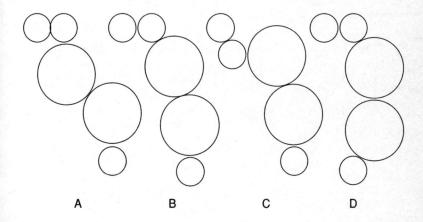

A   B   C   D

10. What letter is missing from the centre?

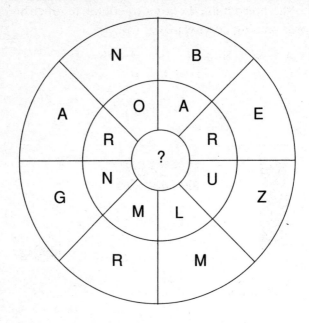

11. What number should replace the question mark?

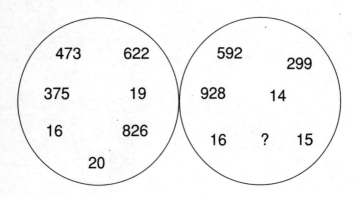

12. The name of which Shakespeare character can be inserted into the bottom line in order to complete nine three-letter words reading downwards?

M	A	W	H	H	H	W	B	S
I	C	A	A	U	I	H	A	E
–	–	–	–	–	–	–	–	–

13.

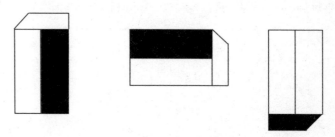

What comes next in the above sequence?

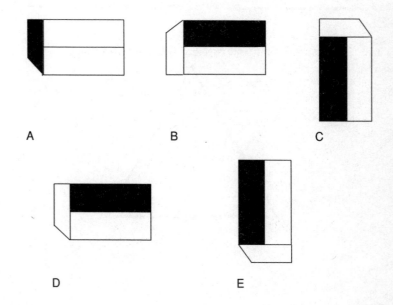

14. Change one letter only from each word to form a well-known phrase:

    AS SHE READS

15. Solve this one-word anagram:

    BARGAIN OIL

16. What number should replace the question mark?

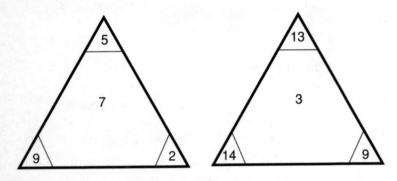

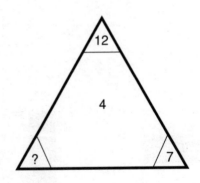

17. Use each letter of the newspaper headline below once each only to spell out the names of three types of fruit.

    No! An Amenable Groan

18. Insert the letters to find two words that form a phrase.

    W L N I S T A T E C N D

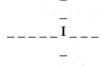

    Clue: peas in a pod.

19. If meat in a river (3 in 6) is T(ham)es, can you find a monkey in church (3 in 6)?

20. Find the starting point and track from letter to adjacent letter horizontally and vertically, but not diagonally, to spell out a 12-letter word. You have to provide the missing letters.

	S	Y	
T	_	A	O
A	S	C	_

21. Place the same four-letter word in front of these words to make new words.
    _ _ _ _HOPPER
    _ _ _ _LET
    _ _ _ _BUD
    _ _ _ _LIKE
    _ _ _ _AGE

22. Find a one-word anagram for TORE GASH.

23. What is a primero?

    a. a card game
    b. a boxer
    c. a rib of beef
    d. a singer

24. What is the name given to a group of rooks?

    a. host
    b. clamour
    c. brood
    d. chattering

25. Find a 10-letter word by moving from circle to circle; you may only use each circle once.

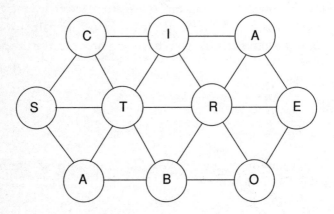

26. Fill in the blanks to find two words that are synonyms.

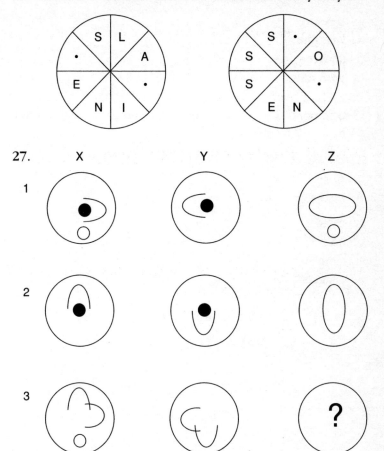

27.

Which circle should replace the question mark?

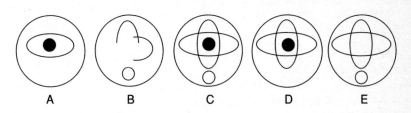

28. Which is the odd one out?

    a. hexagon
    b. pyramid
    c. square
    d. pentagon

29. Place two four-letter bits together to make an eight-letter word.

    AMPO ALIS LURE DENT TANT GREN SELE DEVO IRRI DINE

30. What is a drogger?

    a. castle
    b. boat
    c. caravan
    d. druggist

31. What is the next number in this series?

    −3, +6, +2, −3, +7, −12, ?

32. Find the odd one out.

    BARBEL
    ANABAS
    BARBET
    BELUGA
    GRILSE
    GURNET

33. Fill in the blanks to find two words that are antonyms.

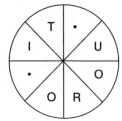 

34.

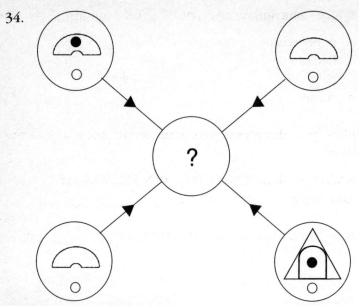

Each line and symbol that appears in the four outer circles, above, is transferred to the centre circle according to these rules. If a line or symbol occurs in the outer circles:

once: it is transferred
twice: it is possibly transferred
3 times: it is transferred
4 times: it is not transferred

Which of the circles A, B, C, D or E, shown below, should appear at the centre of the diagram, above?

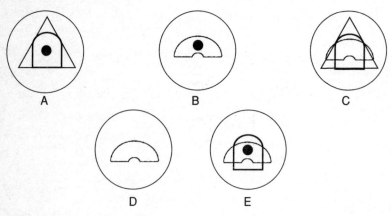

35. Which of the following is always part of comfit?

    a. peppercorns
    b. bacon
    c. ham
    d. sugar

36. Place two three-letter bits together to make a six-letter word.

    SPI, TLE, BUB, ANT, WOR, DAR, MIN, BEE, WAS, LER
    Clue: insect.

37. Which of these is not found in the kitchen?

    CUGPEG
    CIJRUE
    RAGRET
    DIGBRE
    LACSSE

38. Fill in the missing vowels to make a trite saying.

    TRSTV RYBDY BTLWY SCTTH CRDS

39. What word is indicated below?

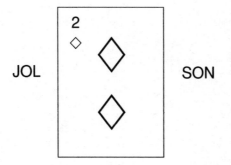

40. Fill in the blanks to find a word.

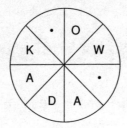

Test Eight: Answers

1. D; the black triangle affixes itself to each arm in turn, the white triangle moves backwards and forwards between two positions, the triangle with the dot moves to each end of the middle arm (above then below) in turn, and the circle moves clockwise to each internal corner in turn.

2. 8 kg; 16/2 = 8

3. highland

4. intricate, simple

5.

A M B I	T E M G	I Y C H
T A A O	O M W O	E E M O
F R T D	N O I O	X F E L

The word *melodramatic* is spelt out round the outside perimeter.

6. D; the others are all the same figure rotated.

7. In 12 months' time.

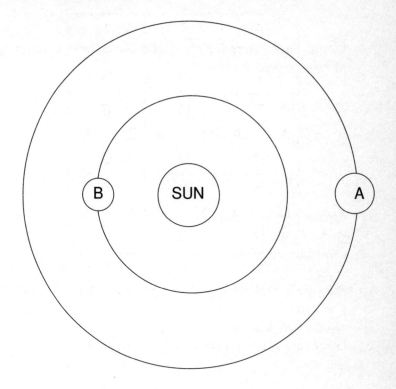

8. take the bull by the horns

9. A; large circles turn to small, and vice versa.

10. E; so that each line of letters produces an anagram of a colour: amber, green, azure, lemon.

11. 10; each two-figure number is the sum of the digits of one of the three-figure numbers in the opposite circle.

12. Desdemona; to give: mid, ace, was, had, hue, him, who, ban, sea.

13. D; the figure rotates 90° at each stage and a different portion is shaded in turn.

14. at the ready

15. aboriginal

16. 16; 12 + 16 = 28/7 = 4

17. banana, lemon, orange

18. identical twins

19. ch(ape)l

20. satisfactory; add the letters i, f, t and r.

21. leaf

22. shortage

23. a. card game

24. b. clamour

25. aerobatics

26. laziness, slowness

27. E; x is added to y to make z, 1 is added to 2 to make 3, but similar symbols disappear.

28. b. pyramid (it is a solid, the rest are polygons).

29. irritant

30. b. boat

31. +12. There are two series: +5 and -9
    -3, +2, +7, +12
    +6, -3, -12

32. Barbet = dog; all the others are fish.

33. timorous, fearless

34. C

35. d. sugar

36. beetle

37. bridge; the others are: eggcup, juicer, grater, scales.

38. Trust everybody but always cut the cards.

39. cardinal

40. workaday

Test Nine: Questions

1. What numbers should replace the question marks?

2	6	30	?
3	5	11	?

2. Which is the odd one out?

   incumbent, obligatory, intrinsic, imperative, irremissible

3. What number should replace the question mark?

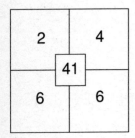 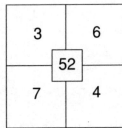 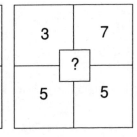

4. Which is the odd one out?

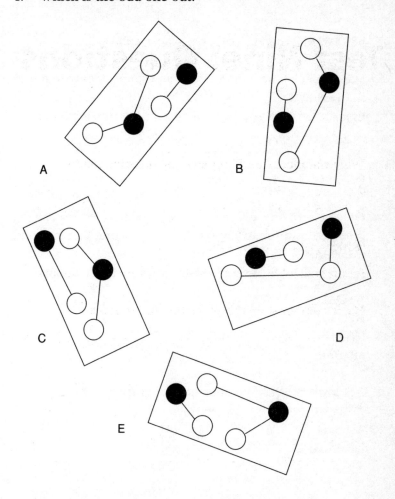

A

B

C

D

E

5. Newton is to force as kelvin is to:

frequency, pressure, light, temperature, sound

6. WRY SARAH is an anagram of which two words that are opposite in meaning?

7. Which word in brackets is closest in meaning to the word in capitals?

   ERSTWHILE (notable, incorrect, near, cultured, past)

8. Start at one of the corner letters and spiral clockwise round the perimeter, finishing at the middle letter, to spell out a nine-letter word. You have to provide the missing letters.

_	N	O
T	E	_
R	O	P

9. Only one of the following groups of five letters can be arranged to form an English five-letter word. Can you find the word?

   MERDO
   HYOAL
   NFOLE
   HURSN
   MUDAP

10. Insert the following words into the grid opposite:

ADROIT	ALAS	TAP
DEMAND	ASIA	ASK
	DESK	ADO
	BIND	ADD
	CHOP	MUD
	ROLE	ACT

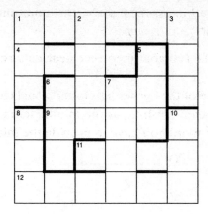

11.

Which square below has most in common with the square above?

A   B   C   D   E

12. What number should replace the question mark in the bottom left-hand triangle?

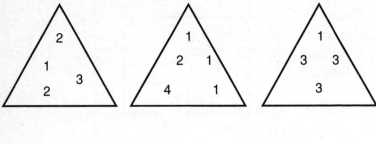

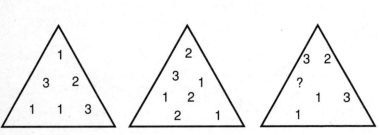

13. Insert two letters in each bracket so that they finish the word on the left and start the word on the right. The letters, when read downwards in pairs, will spell out an eight-letter word.

TA (＿＿) IP
DU (＿＿) SE
DI (＿＿) CH
SO (＿＿) LY

14. Which word is the odd one out?

    carried
    foolish
    scarlet
    quarter
    mansion
    fishing

15. Solve this one-word anagram:

    STAR COUPLE

16.

is to:

as

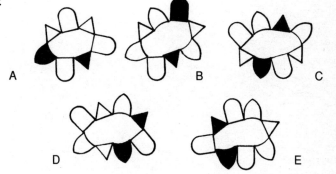

is to:

A B C

D E

17. Which two letters should replace the question marks?

    A   W   F   N   ?
    Z   C   S   J   ?

18. Which is the odd one out?
    RE500
    50I1000E
    NA5Y
    TA101
    GO50500
    B50UE

19. What number should replace the question mark?

    492, 366, 189, 810, ?

20.

What comes next in the above sequence?

A

B

C

D

E

F

21. What is a cairn?

a. a loch
b. a valley
c. a heap of stones
d. an outlook post

22. What have all these words in common?

    bartered
    timepiece
    patrician
    donated
    alfresco

23. What is a peruke?

    a. umbrella
    b. ice cream
    c. wig
    d. flower

24. What is the name given to a group of sheldrake?

    a. dopping
    b. bury
    c. convocation
    d. cloud

25. What number should replace the question mark?

8	2	5	38
7	4	9	59
6	3	7	39
5	1	7	?

26. Fill in the blanks to find two words that are synonyms.

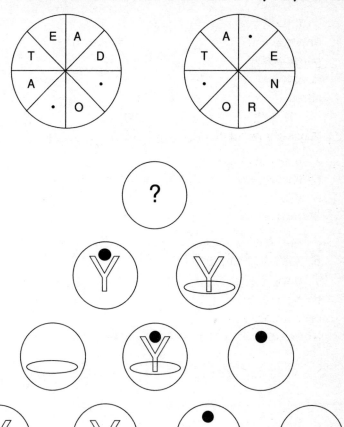

27.

Which circle below should replace the question mark?

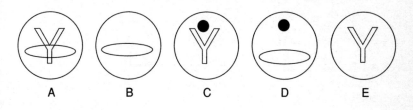

A   B   C   D   E

28. Which of the following is not a cloud?

    a. cumulus
    b. stratus
    c. fumerole
    d. nimbus

29. Add vowels to make a trite saying.

    LLWRK NDNPL YMNSY MKMNY HNDVR FST

30. Find a six-letter word using only these four letters: W O N I

31. What is a fogle?

    a. musical instrument
    b. silk handkerchief
    c. hat
    d. shoes

32. What familiar phrase is suggested below?

33. Find the missing number.

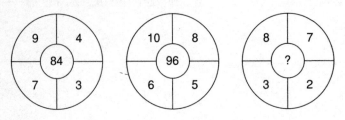

34.

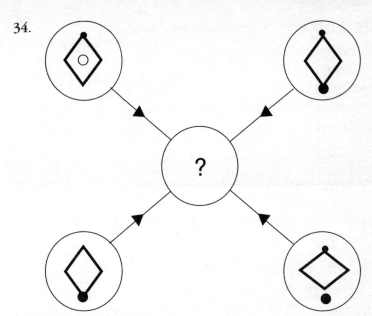

Each line and symbol that appears in the four outer circles, above, is transferred to the centre circle according to these rules. If a line or symbol occurs in the outer circles:

once: it is transferred
twice: it is possibly transferred
3 times: it is transferred
4 times: it is not transferred

Which of the circles A, B, C, D or E, shown below, should appear at the centre of the diagram, above?

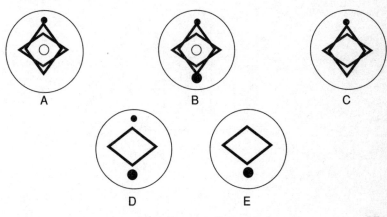

35. Which of the following is not an insect?

    GIAWER
    BASRAC
    SETEST
    RUBLEO
    THENOR

36. Find the missing number.

    ⅞, 1⅜, ?, 2⅜, 2⅞

37. Place two three-letter bits together to make a six-letter word.

    LIA PAN FOD DAH AST SIE DAF TUL IPE ERR
    Clue: flower.

38. Insert a word that means the same as the words outside the brackets.

    BOUNDARY (_ _ _ _) LAKE

39. Place the numbers 11 to 25 in the square so that each horizontal line, vertical line and the two diagonal lines all add up to 65.

	6		8	
			9	5
	7	1		
3				2
10			4	

40. Find the 10-letter word.

    _R_D_I_G_Y

Test Nine: Answers

1. 330 and 41. Multiply the two numbers of the previous pair together to obtain the top number, and add the same two numbers to get the bottom number. So, $30 \times 11 = 330$, $30 + 11 = 41$.

2. intrinsic; it is necessary because it is something that forms an essential part of a whole; the rest are necessary as a duty.

3. 75; $5 \times 75 = 375$. Similarly $7 \times 52 = 364$.

4. D; in all the others a black circle is in the middle of the chain of three connected circles.

5. temperature

6. wary, rash

7. past

8. opportune; add the letters p and u.

9. NFOLE = felon

10.

¹A	D	²R	O	I	³T
⁴C	H	O	P	⁵A	A
T	⁶A	L	⁷A	S	P
⁸M	⁹D	E	S	K	¹⁰A
U	O	¹¹B	I	N	D
¹²D	E	M	A	N	D

11. B; it has lateral symmetry, in other words if the square was cut from top to bottom down the middle, the two halves (left and right) would be identical.

12. 3; the numbers in successive triangles add up to 8, 9, 10, 11, 12, 13.

13. skeleton

14. foolish; all the other words start and finish with consecutive letters of the alphabet, eg, *carried*.

15. speculator

16. D; the figures are in the same order around the body.

17. O and H. There are two sequences going from top to bottom of the columns as follows:

AbCdeFghiJklmnO, and ZyxWvutSrqpoNmlkjiH.

18. TA101; substitute Roman numerals for numbers to read: red, lime, navy, gold and blue. TA101 spells TAXI (10 = X and I = 1).

19. 88; $8 \times 1 = 8, 8 + 0 = 8$

20. B. Reverse each line and discard the third figure from the end each time.

21. c. a heap of stones

22. They all commence with a boy's name: Bart, Tim, Pat, Don, Alf.

23. c. wig

24. a. dopping

25. 34. The first column is multiplied by the third column, and the second column deducted: $(5 \times 7) - 1 = 34$.

26. advocate, attorney

27. D. The lower circles' symbols combine to form the circle above, but similar symbols disappear.

28. c. fumerole

29. All work and no play means you make money hand over fist.

30. winnow

31. b. silk handkerchief

32. a state of confusion

33 $84; (7 \times 4) \times 9/3 = 84; (6 \times 8) \times 10/5 = 96; (3 \times 7) \times 8/2 = 84.$

34. B

35. Rubleo (rouble). The others are: earwig, scarab, tsetse, hornet.

36. 1⅞ (+ ½)

37. dahlia

38. mere

39.

17	6	12	8	22
24	13	14	9	5
11	7	1	25	21
3	23	18	19	2
10	16	20	4	15

40. grudgingly

Test Ten: Questions

1.

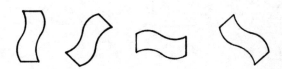

What comes next in the above sequence?

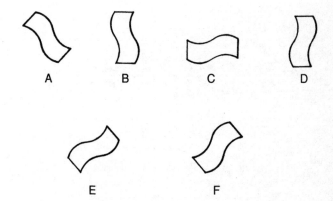

2. How many minutes is it before 12 noon if 20 minutes ago it was three times as many minutes after 9 am?

3. Which word in brackets is closest in meaning to the word in capitals?

    GLUTINOUS (sad, cohesive, voracious, hungry, flushed)

4. INSECURE PET is an anagram of which two words that are opposite in meaning?

5.

Which option below continues the above sequence?

A   B   C

D   E

6. Which is the odd one out?

   nylon, vicuna, acrylic, polyester, acetate

7. Which two words that sound alike but are spelt differently, mean: essence, individual?

8. Which two rhyming words mean: trading residence?

9.

 is to:

as

is to:

    A   B   C   D   E   F

10. What number should replace the question mark?

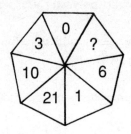

11. A well-known phrase has been divided up into groups of three letters, which have then been placed in the wrong order. Find the phrase:

ATO, EAC, INR, LIK, NAH, OOF, OTT

12. Start at one of the corner letters and spiral clockwise round the perimeter, finishing at the centre letter, to spell out a nine-letter word. You must provide the missing letters.

A   _   E
R   E   _
O   P   A

13.

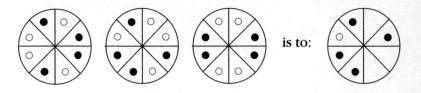

is to:

as

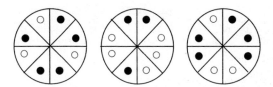

is to:

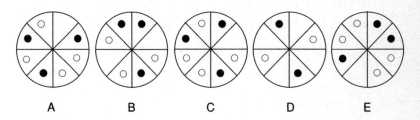

A   B   C   D   E

14. What is the longest English word that can be created using these letters once each only?

IFTWENPAML

15. Which number is the odd one out?

    681422
    751217
    941319
    831114
    391221
    691524
    791625

16. Use every letter of the newspaper headline below, once each only, to spell out the names of three kinds of vegetable.

    Chairperson Can Bat!

17. Which set of letters is the odd one out?

    ADE
    ILM
    RUV
    EHI
    VYZ
    JLM
    FIJ

18.

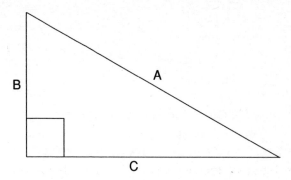

Pythagorean numbers occur when $a^2 = b^2 + c^2$, for example, $34^2 = 16^2 + 30^2$. Find another set of whole Pythagorean numbers where b also equals 16.

19. Complete the three words so that the same two letters that finish the first word start the second, the same two letters that finish the second word start the third and the same two letters that finish the third word also start the first word, thus completing the circle.

_ _ D U _ _
_ _ R E _ _
_ _ L U _ _

20. Insert two letters in each bracket so that they finish the word on the left and start the word on the right. The letters, when read downwards in pairs, will spell out an eight-letter word.

NA (_ _) S H
SA (_ _) S P
CA (_ _) E M
R E (_ _) C H

21. What is the name given to a group of foxes?

    a. earth
    b. dryft
    c. nye
    d. walk

22. Find a one-word anagram for FLAT ROMP.

23. Find a six-letter word using only these four letters: L B U E.

24. What is a papillon?

    a. dog
    b. flower
    c. insect
    d. butterfly

25. What word is represented below?

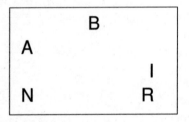

26. Find a 10-letter word by moving from circle to circle; you may only use each circle once.

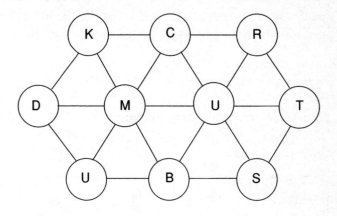

27. Each of the nine squares in the grid marked 1A to 3C should incorporate all the lines and symbols that are shown in the squares of the same letter and number immediately above and to the left. For example, 2B should incorporate all the lines and symbols that are in 2 and B.

One of the squares is incorrect. Which one is it?

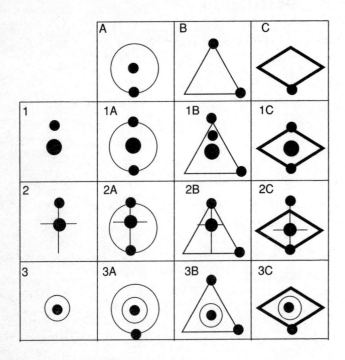

28. Place two four-letter bits together to equal an eight-letter word.

ATES, SLIM, PARE, ORIC, COMP, OMEN, INGO, METE, ORIT, SENT

29. Place the same four-letter word in front of these words to make new words.

    _ _ _ _ WORK
    _ _ _ _ WARE
    _ _ _ _ ORE
    _ _ _ _ CLAD
    _ _ _ _ SMITH

30. Which of these is not a material?

    HARIMO
    TUBRET
    NETEAS
    SKAMAD
    LICOCA

31. A trite saying by Jenkinson.

    H JMZPS UCAIV XCPRN PALCM OQZVS UCCLV XTAIN
    PLACQ SMAPJ LSSAM

    Hint: the answer is unseen, but not much chance of it being OK!

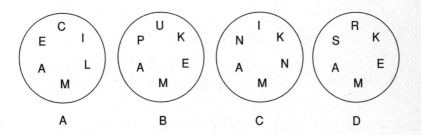

A	B	C	D

32. Which circle cannot be made into a six-letter word?

33. Fill in the blanks to find two words that are synonyms.

 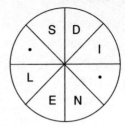

34.

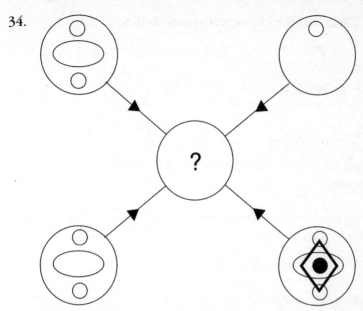

Each line and symbol that appears in the four outer circles, above, is transferred to the centre circle according to these rules. If a line or symbol occurs in the outer circles:

once: it is transferred
twice: it is possibly transferred
3 times: it is transferred
4 times: it is not transferred

Which of the circles A, B, C, D or E, shown below, should appear at the centre of the diagram, above?

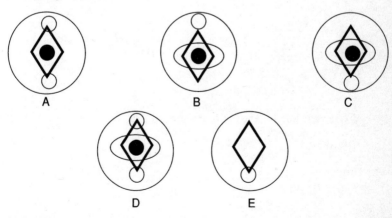

35. Which word is the opposite of pellucid?

    a. fragile
    b. clean
    c. opaque
    d. broken

36. Which two words mean the same?

    surprise, anger, felicity, benevolent, desire, bliss, delicate, stormy

37. All of the vowels have been removed from this trite saying. This is 'Cole's law'.

    THNLY SLCDC BBG

38. What is a melange?

    a. card game
    b. mixture
    c. caramel
    d. ice cream

39. Fill in the blanks and find two words that are synonyms.

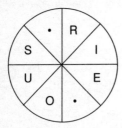 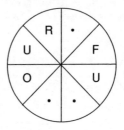

40. What familiar foodstuff is indicated below?

    CROISSA

Test Ten: Answers

1. D; the figure is rotating 45° clockwise at each stage.

2. 40 minutes, or 11.20 am.

3. cohesive

4. erect, supine

5. B; at each stage the black element moves clockwise, first by one space, then two, then three, etc.

6. vicuna; it is a natural material, the rest are man-made.

7. soul/sole

8. selling dwelling

9. C; the top bit folds down into the square, and the bottom bit folds up into it.

10. 15; start at 0 and jump two segments each time clockwise in the sequence: 0 (+ 1) 1 (+ 2) 3 (+ 3) 6 (+ 4) 10 (+ 5) 15 (+ 6) 21.

11. like a cat on a hot tin roof

12. evaporate; add the letters v and t.

13. A; only dots which appear twice in the same segment in the previous three circles are carried forward.

14. filament

15. 941319; in all the others the first two digits are added together to obtain the third and fourth digits, and the second digit is added to the third and fourth digits to obtain the fifth and sixth digits. For example, with 681422, $6 + 8 = 14 + 8 = 22$.

16. spinach, carrot, bean

17. JLM; in all the others there are two spaces in the alphabet between the first two letters and no space between the last two, eg, AbcDE.

18. $65^2 = 16^2 + 63^2$

19. reduce, cereal, allure

20. megastar

21. a. earth

22. platform

23. bubble

24. a. dog

25. scatterbrain

26. dumbstruck

27. 2C

28. meteoric

29. iron

30. butter. The others are: mohair, sateen, damask, calico.

31. It won't work. Read the letter between the letters which follow: ie, H (i) JMZPS (t) UCAIV (w).

32. C. The others are: malice, makeup, makers.

33. imposing, splendid

34. C

35. c. opaque

36. felicity, bliss

37. thinly sliced cabbage

38. b. mixture

39. grievous, mournful

40. shortbread